Praise for
WHEN DOING IT ALL IS UNDOING YOU

"Alyssa Bethke has written a book that is a siren's song for so many of us—calling us all to a reality that is hard to face but important to name and then giving us the peaceful and powerful way out of the rhythms we have each embraced that do not serve us in health or joy. This book is a necessary read for every woman wondering when it will get easier and if that is even possible. Thank God for the words of this book reminding us of what is possible with God."

—**Annie F. Downs**, *New York Times* bestselling author of *That Sounds Fun*

"Alyssa has written a beautiful book that I am sure will resonate deeply with the hearts of so many women. We are all looking to deal with the anxiety in our life and culture but so many people are looking for quick fixes and worldly solutions. Alyssa gets below the surface and summons us to our deep connection with God and roots us in a resilient vision of life and joy with God. I cannot wait to see the beautiful fruit that comes from this book."

—**Jon Tyson**, pastor of the Church of the City of New York, and author of *The Intentional Father*

"If you long to be more present and at peace but your dreams and to-do lists tell you that you are the one holding all things together, this book will revive your heart and bring the relief you long for. This book ultimately empowers us to trust God with all that He has entrusted to us! What a gift this book is."

—**Jeannie Cunnion**, bestselling author of *Don't Miss Out*

"Typically you have to choose between biblical, vulnerable, and practical—but Alyssa's voice is a rare combination of all three. In this book she issues an invitation on the Father's behalf into deeper rest and durable joy, comes alongside those willing to accept that invitation, and walks them home into fullness of heart. I believe freedom and healing are waiting for all who embark on the journey with her."

—**Dr. Brian McCormack**, executive director
of Breakaway Ministries at Texas A&M University

"In *When Doing It All Is Undoing You*, you will experience a depth of theology that is accessible and livable. Maybe my favorite part of the book are the practical 'spiritual practices' found at the end of each chapter to take the theological principles you've learned from contemplation to cultivation through embodied practice. This is one of those books that you will find yourself returning to routinely, because Alyssa keeps pointing us to one who can truly grant our souls rest—Jesus."

—**Joel Muddamalle**, PhD, director of theology and research at
Proverbs 31 Ministries and author of *The Hidden Peace*

"What do you *really* want? It's a fair question, and in *When Doing It All Is Undoing You,* Alyssa Bethke invites us to let go of what we were never meant to hold/fix/control so that God can satisfy our deepest dreams and desires. This book is a "divine glow-up" for the worn-out and weary; keep a copy in your purse and a box in your car, because you're going to want to give it to all of your friends!"

—**Jodie Berndt**, bestselling author of
Praying the Scriptures for Your Children

"I joined the throngs of people doing more than what I was made to do. Alyssa has words beyond her years for those of us who want to find the peace offering of God within a culture that tells us we need to do everything. This book is your antidote to the chaos of life. It is a cup of water for the weary soul."

—**Sara Hagerty**, bestselling author of *Unseen, The Gift of Limitations*, and *Every Bitter Thing Is Sweet*

WHEN DOING IT ALL IS UNDOING YOU

WHEN DOING IT ALL IS UNDOING YOU

Meeting God in Your Unmet Expectations

Alyssa Joy Bethke

WORTHY
PUBLISHING

New York • Nashville

Worthy

Hachette Book Group

1290 Avenue of the Americas, New York, NY 10104

worthypublishing.com

twitter.com/worthypub

First Edition: September 2024

Worthy is a division of Hachette Book Group, Inc. The Worthy name and logo are registered trademarks of Hachette Book Group, Inc.

The publisher is not responsible for websites (or their content) that are not owned by the publisher.

The Hachette Speakers Bureau provides a wide range of authors for speaking events. To find out more, go to hachettespeakersbureau.com or email HachetteSpeakers @hbgusa.com.

Worthy Books may be purchased in bulk for business, educational, or promotional use. For information, please contact your local bookseller or the Hachette Book Group Special Markets Department at special.markets@hbgusa.com.

Library of Congress Cataloging-in-Publication Data has been applied for.

ISBNs: 978-1-5460-3408-7 (hardcover); 978-1-5460-3409-4 (e-book)

Printed in the United States of America

LSC-C

Printing 1, 2024

To Kinsley, Kannon, and Lucy

May you boldly and passionately follow Jesus as you continue to entrust Him with your heart and find His to be trustworthy and true. May you walk with Him, look to Him, and radiate with His light and love.

I love you forever and ever.

What matters is not the accomplishments you achieve; what matters is the person you become.

—DALLAS WILLARD

CONTENTS

INTRODUCTION

I woke up at 5:30 yesterday morning and shuffled into the kitchen, eyes half-opened, my hair all askew. I steamed my oat milk. I pulled my shot of coffee and drizzled some maple syrup in that cup of pure joy and walked back into my dark room. I fell into my lounge chair, clicked on the lamp, and began to journal.

While sipping my latte, I wrote to the Lord, giving thanks for the last ten days, for how He had carried me while my husband, Jeff, had been away on a work trip and I was solo parenting. I had planned to work and study and "mom" during that time, but my babysitter got sick for the week, my mom (who is such a help to me and lives near us) came down with the flu, and I caught it as well. However, as I shifted gears and slowed, accepting my week as it was instead of how I'd planned it, the Lord carried me in the sweetest of ways.

I was able to rest with Lucy, our four-year-old, during the days while the two bigs were at school. We watched shows, played doll-house, crafted, and spent time outside. My sickness was not the "can't get out of bed" kind, so I was able to be fully present to my kids. I even made homemade cinnamon rolls (a rare occurrence for me)! It was a gentle week. A week of rest, of being present, of not being hurried or worried. There were no *should*s in my head; I had been forced to let them go. But there was an invitation for me to let my soul rest in Jesus, who takes care of me as I took care of my family.

And I was amazed. It was a work of God. For years, whenever Jeff went away, I would fall into the loop of anxiety and exhaustion, struggling to manage it all. But for the first time—seriously, the first time in nine years of motherhood—I welcomed the solo parenting and embraced the new rhythm as I walked at the pace of Jesus, trying to go slow and be present.

Now, before you think, *This gal has no idea what it's like to be me! This is not my reality*, just you wait. I share that to say this is what it *can* be like. This is what I believe the Lord wants to offer us: an invitation for rest, joy, love, and peace in the midst of whatever reality you are facing.

Later, I met my good friend at the park with our three littles. As they scampered around, climbing and swinging and giggling, we stood in the middle of that playground, sharing our hearts— talking about how we were really doing and letting the pain and anxiety bubble up and over.

Through tears, she shared how she felt like she couldn't find her footing. A recent transition had left her wobbly, and it seemed like she couldn't catch her breath, that nothing was sticking. She wondered about this season. She admitted to being snappy with her husband. Critical.

"I can be critical of Jeff when I start to feel worthless," I admitted. "'Don't you see all that I am doing? Can you thank me for all that I am carrying?' I often say to him."

Through tears, she said, "Yes, that's it. I feel worthless. What's my purpose?"

My heart broke. Oh, how I know the feeling of worthlessness.

Often, I don't consciously realize that's what I'm feeling, but when I'm able to name it, it's as if I get punched in the stomach.

That night, after we picked Jeff up from the airport with shouts and *hoorays* from the kids (and me!), we sat around the dinner table eating orange chicken and digging into Straus's maple cream ice cream (Have you had it? It's unbelievable. Autumn in your mouth!) sprinkled with the maple crunchies Jeff brought home from Vermont. Soon, everyone else was fast asleep in their beds, and I was gearing up for some hours of study on the couch for my seminary class the next day. I was halfway done with my master's, and I was loving every moment of learning and studying the Bible—a dream come true for me.

For the past months, I had chosen to fast from social media so I could really focus on this book and hear what the Lord wanted to speak to me. (And truth be told, I did not have that much margin in my life with school and writing. I wouldn't necessarily recommend doing both at the same time!) However, I had a few minutes to spare (okay, let's call it what it was—procrastination), and I really wanted to catch up on the latest with Taylor Swift's love life. (Listen, I am the most uncultured person you will ever meet—true "grandma" status here with culture and technology. However, Taylor and I go way back to when her *Fearless* album had just come out and I would blast her song "Love Story" on my blue iPod while I cleaned the church's bathrooms and dance with the mop, wishing it were Jeff, who, at the time, I was dating long-distance.) I swiped my phone up and clicked on that little app. It sucked me in like quicksand.

They're in Europe!
She's coming out with a new podcast!
She's coming out with a book!
She had a party tonight!

Look at her new house—wow!

She's pregnant!

It wasn't until ten minutes had passed that I realized I hadn't even searched for Taylor Swift (priorities, people). Finally, I looked up at the time, put my phone away, and grabbed my seminary book.

I sat down on the couch with a brownie in hand and let out a big sigh.

I couldn't concentrate on my book. I was excited for everyone's updates on social media, truly. I knew the hard work that went into each project. So many of the announcements were answers to prayer, evidence of years of waiting and dreaming. I had prayed with a lot of those friends for those very desires.

And yet, within a matter of minutes, I felt like my journal pages from that morning had been wiped away.

What am I doing with my life? What do I have to show for my season? Who am I? What's my purpose? Have I been wasting my life?

I felt insecure, unseen, and—here's that word—worthless. I was falling behind. I was missing it somehow. Shame came knocking at my door, and I let it walk right on in.

Now, this is not a book about social media. And although my examples from this particular day involve my roles as a wife and mom, I am sure that in whatever season of life you are living right now, you can relate to feeling worthless and purposeless, to falling into the comparison trap, to feeling insecure and disappointed with life. To feeling that this life is not what you thought it would be, not only that it's harder, but that no matter what you try, you can feel yourself unravel at times—in the big things of life and the small moments of our everyday.

I know many of you can relate to feeling just flat-out exhausted from trying to manage the outcomes and the reality that life is not going the way you had hoped. If you're like me, you may find yourself struggling to know how to proceed, or to know what yours is to do, and to let go of holding your life and situations so tightly out of fear of everything falling apart. If we let go, will we fall apart?

What I am arguing for in this book is our hearts. More than the outcomes, more than the situations themselves or even the endings to our stories; what about who we are becoming in the midst of all that is left undone? When it comes to "keeping up with the Joneses," breathing the air of our culture and walking in the demands and pressures of our day is insurmountably exhausting. Because I hadn't been on the 'Gram in so long, it was extremely apparent how quickly my heart swung from thankfulness and joy in the morning to insecurity and questions and doubts and—let's just say it—jealousy late that night. And it's not that social media causes those things in me, but rather it highlights the areas of my heart that are already broken.

The areas of my life that cause me to feel like I'm in pieces and that leave me weary and feeling forgotten.

And my first response was not to run to the Father but to do something amazing! Insta-worthy. I felt the pressure to prove myself. Show myself. Which then quickly faded into self-pity.

But do I have anything to show?

As I sat on my oversized gray couch, having completely demolished my brownie, I was fighting to preach to myself the very truth I'd shared with my friend at the playground earlier that day:

Alyssa, it's not about what you accomplish or do. Yes, we're made to partner with God in doing good works to bring His light to the world, but the most important gift you can give to people is your presence, your transformed self. Who are you? Who are you becoming? It's not about your resume; it's about your heart.

I had shared with my friend that day that when I think of the most influential people in my life, my family and mentors who have helped shape me, I don't think about their resumes. It's not the things they've done that have changed my life. It's *who* they are while they spend time with me that sticks with me—how they listen, look me in the eye, ask questions, make me feel like they have all the time in the world and are delighted to be with me. It's their posture of kindness, grace, and love. It's how they speak into my life, the wisdom and grace and truth that they share. How they pray over and for me. How they pursue me. How they are available. How they follow up to see how I'm doing with the burdens and cares that I share with them. It's their very presence, their transformed selves, their whole and holy selves. It's that they too are on the journey of seeking to be full of Jesus and choosing to be fully devoted to Jesus. That is their gift to me.

The same is true of me. Of you. Of each one of us.

It's not about what we accomplish, although we're made to do good, but it's who we are *becoming* that is the most important.

Now, we can become many things. We are always being formed. The question is what and who are you looking to reflect? We can become like the world, and the more we look to it and fill our minds with it, the more like it we will be. And the more unsteady and ungrounded we will become. Or we can become more like Jesus, as we look to Him and spend time with Him and surround ourselves with other people who are faithfully walking with Him. And as we become like Jesus, we actually become our truest selves, people who are full of grace, love, joy, and peace.

It's us looking to Him, and Him looking at us. With no fear. No shame. No guilt. But total love and delight.

Becoming more like Jesus means opening up our hearts to God, connecting with Him, and connecting with others in community and generously serving. It's about being transformed, full of His goodness and grace and glory.

And that goodness and grace and glory are what change the atmospheres and spheres of the places we reside. No, we can't change people or control them or manage the outcomes of what happens in our lives, but we can choose how we show up and how we love and how we respond. Our job is to look to Jesus, to be devoted to Him and His Word, to ask to be filled more and more with His Spirit and to obey Him. As we walk this out, looking and longing for Jesus, we will in turn become more like Him: soft hearted, gentle, compassionate, courageous, bold, secure, and full of joy because we will be people who have a peaceful presence, knowing He is God and we are not, and that is good news. We will no longer be anxious, worried, fearful, or controlling. But this is not a one time thing. This is not a "do these five steps and you will be a new you!" There is not a way to fast track your formation or to control or manipulate God. This is a daily choosing to look to Jesus, to form small habits that take your heart and mind off of the things you can control and to step into His presence and to receive all that He has, all that He is, in His way. It is a journey. A process. A relationship with the King of Kings and the One who cares deeply for you.

This book is about my journey of being brought to the end of myself, undone, and having God put me back together. It's a story of me going from complete exhaustion and stress from trying to manage the outcomes of my life and my people to no avail to one of learning to seek God in the secret place and letting His love transform me. It is a story of learning to let go of the results and live with loose ends while still living with hope and peace. It is a story of how God wants to replace our weariness with restored peace by weaving love and joy into the depths of your soul, right in the midst of your very reality, in the midst of the mess, the pain, the suffering, the hurt. And here's the beauty: our coming apart isn't something to run away from or feel shame over, but rather it's the exact place where God wants us to be so He can put us back together. When we feel undone, or something in our life is crumbling to pieces, whether a big thing or a day-to-day thing that we cannot control or change, it's actually an invitation from the Lord to come to Him, *come again*, and be desperately dependent on Him to not put it back together, but to put *us* back together.

And although I've come a long way and want to show you how you can too, I have not arrived. My transformation is not "done and dusted," as my favorite Peloton instructor, Leanne Hainsby, says. Our spiritual journey is just that—a journey. It is a process, a slow growth, a long obedience in the same direction, as Eugene Peterson would say.[1] Obviously, I am still in formation. I am still hit with the temptations to do more and be more. I am still hit with the hard burdens of life that leave me wanting to give up and get out. I still have situations in my life that I can't control or change, and the pain of them hits so tenderly at times that I am left crying out to God as my constant tears stain my journal pages.

But the difference is that I go to God instead of trying to figure it out on my own. I know that God is after my heart. That He not only cares for my heart in the roller coaster of life, but that He goes before me and holds all things together, including my very soul. He takes the disintegrated and integrates it. He takes the pieces and makes a masterpiece. He plants our feet on holy ground, fills us with His presence, and lets His love flow through us. And He reminds me over and over that I am in Christ, and He delights in me, and He is authoring a beautiful story in and through me. Yes, my story may not end the way I hope, but He is weaving me together with His careful and gentle precision and drawing me deeper into His presence and filling me with His power to be a gift to others.

I see a pattern in so many women today. I see it so clearly in my own life, too. In addition to everything else we're trying to manage, we're also trying so hard to manage our hearts. The pattern usually looks something like this:

1. We **neglect** our hearts. Life gets too busy, we get too hurt, and we don't know what to do with all that we feel or experience and simply don't have the energy to go "there," so we neglect them. Shut them down. Stuff our unwanted feelings down. Ignore.

2. We try to **earn** our hearts. Life feels out of control and scary so we do all that we can to protect them and find strength for our hearts in our own way on our own strength. We reach out for some kind of formula for life, try to find the handbook or the rule that will protect us or flip the script. We want success and happiness and to avoid pain at all costs, so we try to do the five steps to feel worthy and loved and known and safe.

3. We **lose** heart. We are hit with the reality that no matter what goal we set, what dream or longing we have or how intentional we are, life does not go the way we wanted it or thought. The formula, the rule, isn't working. Life is too hard. Too painful. The wait too long. And so we grow weary and exhausted and don't know how much longer we can hold out. We can become disillusioned when it doesn't go the way we expected it to.

Sometimes we cycle through these three aspects, and sometimes the path is more linear.

All three of these ways of relating to life are human. Sometimes we cannot take the pain all at once, so we need to tread slowly into healing. Pain and loss are scary. We long to be protected. Life not living up to our expectations and ideals can be extremely disheartening.

And the world gives us no tools for facing pain or unmet expectations and outcomes. The world shouts that life is all about outcomes. It's all about accomplishments and what is seen and what you have to show for all your hard work. Life is about happiness and ease. Things going your way. (And if they don't go your way, then you make a way.)

But I think God has something far greater for us. He is inviting us into a life lived with **fullness of heart.**

This book is a look at the ways we neglect and try to earn our hearts and how so often we lose heart and how God is offering us a better way. What does it look like to have fullness of heart? And can we have that in the midst of pain and responsibility and longing? Can we actually be honest about all the heavy burdens we have stuffed down in our hearts? About our disappointments and unmet longings and hurts? Can we actually go there? And how? *Won't I come apart even more if I go there?*

What if going there with Jesus is the one thing you need to be set free? And what if you're met with such tenderness and gentleness that causes your heart not only to be set free, but to be safely placed in the Father's faithful and trustworthy hands? That's what I want to explore together. I have broken this book up into four sections. In the first section, we will see how we often neglect our hearts and focus on what we can do by trying to grasp for control, but finding that just leaves us exhausted. We'll talk about how often we aren't even aware of what's going on inside of us. We'll also look at how to decipher between our desires, and we'll look at how you are made for so much more.

In the second section, we move into chapters about how we try to gain heart, grasping for ways we can find strength. Often when things surface that are uncomfortable, we try to control, please, and balance. We want to fix them, ease them, and please them.

The third section is about what happens when we lose heart. We've tried everything, but it's not working. We are hit with the realities of disappointments, griefs, and longings that are not only unfulfilled but often shattered. How do we keep our hearts together and whole? How do we tend our hearts when faced with such hardship and hurt?

The fourth section moves into God's desire for us—to give us fullness of heart. What does it look like to live on this earth with these troubles and responsibilities, with these desires and dreams? What is God's vision for us as women? As people who look to Him? How can we show up to our realities and live—with fullness of love, peace, and joy—regardless of our circumstances or outcomes?

At the end of each chapter, I've included a simple spiritual practice that you can do to connect your heart with God. These are not extensive, but I hope they give you some tools and practices in your belt to pull out each day and stop and connect with God, and to stop and connect with your own heart. I hope you will learn a new rhythm that reminds you that you are not what you do, but you are a child of God whom He greatly delights in and holds in His heart, right where you are today. Spiritual practices have become a huge game changer for me in my journey with Jesus, in knowing Him and hearing from Him. I hope this book gives you a little taste of small ways you can connect with God daily and hear from Him.

I firmly believe that we connect with God with our whole selves—mind, heart, and body. This book focuses primarily on the heart and mind, but please don't forget about your body. It's where God dwells and it is where we host heaven. Walking, dancing, eating, fasting, serving—these are all ways that we connect with God and show God to the world.

I pray that this book will show you that your heart matters. I pray you will know God better by the end of this book and know how to let Him know you by opening up your heart to Him. He is your safe place, your refuge and harbor. He longs to hold you and hold the things on your heart and hold you together. He wove you together in the womb, and He continues to weave hope and joy into your life as you continue to connect with God and entrust your whole self to Him. There is no shame, no guilt, no grief, and no hardship too difficult for God to cleanse, to heal, and to hold. He longs for you to come to Him; He is inviting you to come.

You are a masterpiece. I pray this book strengthens your inner being, that Christ may dwell in your heart through faith, and that you would know the love of the King and be filled with all of His fullness.

> Now to Him who is able to do far more abundantly than all that we ask or think, according to the power at work within us, to him be glory in the church and in Christ Jesus throughout all generations, forever and ever. Amen.
>
> —EPHESIANS 3:20

Grace and peace,

Lyss

PART I

NEGLECTING OUR HEARTS

What is the heart, and does it matter? What does God think of our hearts? How do we care for our hearts when life is busy, hard, and we've been hurt? Sometimes it can be easier to neglect our hearts, to just not go there or tend to it, because we don't know where to start, or how to work through our pain, or why it even matters because we can't always solve it, fix it, or find a solution. Our lives are complex, and confusion can set in, and we can be afraid that if we go there everything might unravel; we might unravel.

Neglecting our hearts can just seem easier.

But what if God has something so much more for us? What if life isn't about all that we do, or what we can show, but more about who we are becoming? What if our hearts are the very thing we need to fully live?

1

EXHAUSTION

I pull on my cozy pajamas and walk into my bathroom. My shoulders feel heavy, my chest tight. Without thinking, I start my nighttime routine. I quickly throw my hair into a messy bun and turn on the faucet. I splash my face with the cold water, holding my hands a little longer over my eyes. It has been such a long day. As I begin to scrub the bubbly soap over my cheeks, I silently go through my checklist for the day, seeing if I did everything I was supposed to. The house is quiet, and my inner voice gets louder.

Oh shoot, I forgot that. I'll do that tomorrow—while I wonder if I can remember.

I need to get that for this week too. Maybe I'll run by Target on Thursday on my way home.

What should I say back to that text? I don't want her to misread it.

Then as I rinse my face and start wiping away the black mascara from my eyes, my mind once again plays the scene I can't stop thinking about. My heart starts to drop; my head slumps as a silent tear rolls down my face. I quickly wash it away with the water.

The voices in my head seem so loud, so constant as I replay the conversation over and over. I think of all the ways I could have responded differently, or what I should have done. I think about the things that I wish were different. If *I* were different. If they were different. The endless loop plays as if I pushed Repeat.

I grab the fuzzy towel next to me and pat my face dry. As I look into the mirror to apply my night cream, I notice my eyes. The spark and light aren't there, not like they used to be.

I take a big breath and sigh.

I grab my phone on the counter and pull up Google as I shuffle to my bed.

"How to..." I type in the search bar. Surely there's a way to crack the code, to help me know what to do.

I shuffle to my bed in the dark and climb under the covers. As I lie there, I scroll, and click, and read each article that comes up. After a while, I click on Instagram, wanting to escape my reality for a bit.

An hour later, as my eyes keep closing on me, I put the phone on my nightstand and fall fast asleep.

Morning comes too soon. Immediately I go through my checklist for the day, before even placing my feet on the ground.

I sit up and sigh. My eyes are struggling to open, my body feels tight, and I stand. "Another day."

How many of my nights, and my mornings, have looked just like that one? It is a constant battle to get off of the hamster wheel of endless things I need to do. My mind can run ragged with not only my checklist, but also my ideas and hopes of what I want to do in a day, or in a season. It also can spiral around with all that didn't go well that day, all that didn't live up to my hopes or ideals. All my disappointments, discouragements, and despairs.

Women bear a lot of responsibility and have been given a lot to care for. We hold a lot in our lives. Jobs, homes, families, relationships. Things need to get done. No matter what season of life you are in, I can guarantee that your arms and your head and your heart are full, caring for others as well as carrying your everyday workload. And I can guess that you give yourself little room to be self-aware of your own needs and heart.

We often talk about women and work-life balance. Women can easily take on lots of responsibilities not only in their jobs, but also in their lives. We can take on many roles, which can leave us feeling worn-out when we don't prioritize the right things and we say yes to too many things.

We also have beautiful ideas for how we want things to be or to go, and I think that's a God-given capacity that we should celebrate. Dreaming of good. Longing for beauty. Wanting joy and peace and love. But often, life can feel so heavy when it doesn't measure up to our dreams, no matter how much we try. It feels like *we* don't measure up.

It gets sticky, and we get stuck when we think it's up to us to fulfill every responsibility, and when we feel the pressure to do it all perfectly. We start trying to control ourselves and others and our circumstances because we are so anxious about what *could* happen or because what *is* happening is too painful.

It gets suffocating when we can't go about our days with freedom and joy, but rather we weigh ourselves down with the expectations of others, or ourselves. We feel heavy laden when we feel the weight of needing to hold everyone else together while wondering why we can't get it together ourselves.

It gets exhausting when we feel like it's up to us to manage all the outcomes.

It's all up to me, we think. We feel alone, isolated, lonely.

And when we fail, or the thing falls apart despite our best efforts, what do we do? Where do we go? Who are we when we don't live up to those expectations? Where is our hope when things don't play out the way we had prayed or longed for? Or how do we carry on when it just seems like things aren't changing for the better?

When, in spite of all our best efforts, it's all in pieces, unable to be mended?

We are left in pieces.

The exhaustion from it all hits us like a ton of bricks. So when we get ready for bed at night, despite our efforts and despite our showing up and doing the thing in front of us, we still feel heavy and anxious and doubtful.

Sissy Goff, in her book *Raising Worry-Free Girls*, talks about the pressure girls are experiencing today. She says, "Girls feel too much pressure—to please, to perform, to excel, to be responsible. Plus, they want to look beautiful while they're doing it all and doing it all well."[1] Although Goff is talking about girls under eighteen here, I find this to also be true of us women today. We are living in unprecedented times, with the internet and social media so much a part of our lives. Never before have other women been able to see what everyone is up to, accomplishing, wearing, and looking like on a daily basis. We are bombarded by possibilities, and opportunities quickly turn into expectations that we feel the weight of living up to.

Not only are there thousands of things to do to succeed, not only are our minds trying to hold all those thousands of things, but we come face-to-face with our limitations and the reality is that we cannot be fully present to all of those things. We can't hold all those things up. But if we don't, who will?

It's too much.

So we feel like everything, and everyone, simply has pieces of us.

And we start to feel like we only have a piece of us.

Fragmented.

Floating.

Weary to the core.

We are exhausted from holding it all together. We are weary from trying to manage all the outcomes.

Women not only hold all the things, but we also carry the emotional weight of it all. Sociologist Arlie Hochschild introduced the concept of emotional labor for women in 1983. She described emotional labor as "a concept that encompasses the effort required to manage and express emotions to meet the expectations of others. It involves managing one's own emotions, recognizing and responding to the emotions of others, and regulating emotional expressions in various social interactions."[2]

We feel the burden of managing not only our own emotions, but the emotions of those around us, whether it's in the office, in our homes, or in any social gathering. We feel like we need to meet others' expectations emotionally, and it can be exhausting.

What will they think of me?

Did I say that right?

Did I come off too strong?

I want to make sure everyone feels seen by me and included.

I don't want to hurt anyone's feelings.

I need to suppress myself because I'm too much.

I'm not sensitive enough and worry about offending them.

We often feel the pressure to not be too much, while also the anxiety of not being enough. We don't want to be too needy, too emotional, too high-maintenance. Will they take us seriously? Will we be a burden? Will we turn them away?

And at the same time, we fear we aren't enough—that we're not smart enough, not capable enough, not able to hold it all together. We try to fit this perfect mold, although we aren't quite sure what that model is that we're trying to emulate. Sometimes we may feel like we have to prove ourselves to be included, while sometimes suffering from imposter syndrome, wondering, "Will they think I'm a fraud?"

Regardless of your personality or wiring, we all as women carry deep within us the emotional weight of our own lives and those that we care about.

I lead a group of women that are all leaders and entrepreneurs. We get together twice a year, and one of the things we always do is something we call "hot seats." We have an hour, and anyone who wants to share can do so. They each have eight minutes on the floor. For the first minute, they share their current challenge or biggest struggle in which they feel stuck and need advice, and for the last seven minutes, we all get to go around and offer insight. Not in-depth, long insight but quick ideas: "Have you thought of this?" "I know someone who can help you—talk to me later." "I think hitting these three topics is key." Jeff also leads a group of men who are all entrepreneurs, and they do this every time they gather as well. Problems are solved. Insight is given. New visions and help are received. They do this for both business and family, and for their personal lives.

Well, the first gathering we had, I tried this with these women talking about our businesses, it went spectacularly. I set my timer for eight minutes, and we all took our turn talking. But the next day when I opened the hot seats for our personal lives, only two women got to go within the hour, and a minute into each one of them sharing, they immediately broke down in tears. I quietly put my timer away, realizing that our personal struggles and challenges as women are not meant to be solved in eight minutes. We are carrying so much, and it's all woven together. Oftentimes, even though we are holding so much—so many desires and longings and pain points of the people around us—we aren't asked often enough, "How are you doing, really?" To be given space to be heard and listened to and encouraged and prayed over is so needed. And to not have it timed, but to have a safe space to process.

When we care for others in this way, we are doing the very thing God asks us to do: Carry each other's burdens (Gal. 6:2); Weep with one another, rejoice with one another (Romans 12:15); Encourage one another (1 Thess. 5:11).

We can do this beautifully, like when we hold a crying child in our arms and listen to their sadness and comfort them. We do this when our friend tells us they met a guy on Hinge over a conversation about meatloaf and he, in fact, turns out to be an amazing man of God, and the whole Bible study group squeals with delight! (True story!) We do this when our sister is grieving over a divorce, and the confusion and hurt and utter devastation seem like they're all too much to bear. And all we can do is listen, cry with them, grieve with them, and pray gut-honest prayers.

We are made to hold each other. To hold the beautiful and to hold the utterly devastating. This is the heart of God, to be moved to compassion.

These are all good.

However, like any good thing, we can also go too far. We can take on others' pain as our own and feel like it's all up to us to make it right. We can feel the pressure to hold everything together and to do all the right things so that no one else falls apart. We can question if we said the right thing, if they misread us or misunderstood us. We can think that if we do it just so, everything will be okay, that no one will freak out or break or struggle.

Emily Jamieson, my prayer warrior and friend who is queen of one-liners, says, "We can be *committed* to others' happiness, but we are *not responsible* for their happiness."

And here's the thing: sometimes I can get so caught up in caring for others that I lose track of how my own heart is doing.

That, mixed with the demands of the day, the demands of the season, with the dreams and goals that I am working toward, means I start to forget about what really matters. I start to think that I am what I can accomplish, not who God says I am. I start to take my eyes off of Jesus and focus them on what everyone else is doing and what I need to be doing, and trying to manage it all.

And instantaneously I start to strive, start to live out of stress and worry and anxiety, instead of living with grace and peace and unhurry. I start to unravel, and my unraveling affects my people.

I completely neglect my soul. I lay it on the altar of doing more and being more. Or sometimes I hide behind good things, like caring for others and serving them but in a way where I'm really looking for my worth and purpose in them.

I start to turn from seeking and loving Jesus with my whole self and seeking to find love for myself in others and other things.

I don't take the time to search my heart, to stop and look at my inner being and bring it before the Lord. I don't take the time to connect with Jesus, to hear from Him, or to simply be with Him because "Watch out, world! I am on a mission—things to do, things to fix, things to prove!"

Until I find myself alone at night, downing chocolate, numbing out to *Gilmore Girls*, trying to stuff down the feelings of loneliness, disconnect, discouragement, and weariness.

I try to fix, so I google.

I try to numb, so I binge-watch.

I try to avoid the pain, so I focus on others.

I try to feel something good, so I shop.

I try to escape, so I swipe.

I get tired of trying, so I shut down and close off.

I look for the formula, thinking this will be the thing that changes everything.

Surely there's a five-step process to avoid this pain. Surely there are three easy things I can do to fix this. Can't there be a way to overcome? A way to find the answer? Something I can do to make it better?

I start to become like the Israelites in the Old Testament who had been slaves in Egypt and kept going back to their old ways. God had sent Moses to "let his people go." (Exod. 5:1) And miraculously, he led a whole nation out of slavery and out from under the demanding rule of Pharaoh (after many plagues and back and forth pleas and unfaithful promises from Pharaoh).

The Israelites had seen miracle after miracle. They had crossed the Red Sea, which had been parted by the Lord's might. They walked right through it (I can't even imagine!), and when the Egyptians chased them down, the waves came crashing in on them.

The Israelites had been freed!

They had been rescued!

They had been liberated from a life of slavery!

And yet, if you keep reading through the Torah, you'll find that they didn't know *how* to live free. They kept going back to other gods, trying to please them, instead of living to please God alone and becoming His "treasured possession" (Exod. 19:5).

They kept living like slaves, wanting to be like the other nations and find security in what they could manipulate. Please understand, the gods of the nations were powerful spiritual beings. The Egyptian magicians were able to turn staffs into snakes by the power of these evil angelic beings (Exod. 7:11–12). There are gods all over the world who have been given authority in different areas (1 Kings 11:5–7, Dan. 10:13, 20). When the Israelites couldn't see God working and moving, they decided they could do something about their problems by worshipping these other gods.

In ancient times, Ba'al and Asherah were the gods of Canaan whom people worshipped and whom the Israelites constantly turned to. (God was after the Israelites' hearts, longing for them to be wholly devoted to Him. People sacrificed their own children to the gods Molek and Ba'al (makes my stomach hurt to think about). And the Israelites turned to these gods because worshipping them seemed more likely to produce the results they wanted than waiting on Yahweh.

The book of Leviticus, which is a long book with a lot of rules (I know, I know!), was written because God wanted the Israelites to put spiritual practices into place to remind themselves of who they really were. They were no longer slaves, identified by what they did or what they could accomplish, but they were children of God, identified by the love of their Father. God had rescued them from slavery in Egypt, but now they had to learn a whole new way of living.

God wanted the Israelites to abandon other gods and draw close to Him. He wants the same for us. Can I tell you a secret about the Bible? It is a beautiful love story of how the triune God created us out of His great love and delight because He wanted to partner with us in bringing His kingdom to earth. He wanted to fight back darkness, to create communities of righteousness and justice with us. Not because He needed us, but because He wanted us. He wanted to be close to us, united, one, intimate. And throughout the Bible, God gets closer and closer to us.

First, He creates the garden and lets man dwell there, and He dwells there with him.

Well, we all know how that went down. Sin entered, perfect union was broken, but God promises the saving Messiah in Genesis 3. Then in Matthew, we first see how Jesus, the Son of God, takes on human flesh and dwells among people. He walks on the earth, He talks, He eats, He serves, He loves, He dies and resurrects. God gets closer. Human flesh and blood.

But then He ascends, as King, sitting at the right hand of God the Father. And He promises the Holy Spirit, who is even better because now God in the Spirit dwells *in* us. Inside of us. In our human bodies!

And He longs to dwell in us to transform us and to make what is invisible visible to the lost world.

This is a story of love, of intimacy, of allegiance in our hearts to the King of the universe.

And where does He reside? In our hearts.

He longs to take up residence within us, to fill us, but how can He when we make no room for Him? How can He indwell us when all the doors of our heart are shut off to Him, shut off to others, shut off to our own selves? How can He when our hearts are so burdened? And yet, when we are so exhausted, so weary, and we feel like our hearts are coming undone, that is exactly when God wants to restore us and mend us back together so He can fully fill us with His presence.

Matthew 11:28–30 in *The Message* (which is one of my favorite translations of this verse) says, "Are you tired? Worn out? Burned out on religion? Come to me. Get away with me and you'll recover your life. I'll show you how to take a real rest. Walk with me and work with me—watch how I do it. Learn the unforced rhythms of grace. I won't lay anything heavy or ill-fitting on you. Keep company with me and you'll learn to live freely and lightly."

Dane Ortlund, in his book *Gentle and Lowly*, explains this verse, saying,

> You don't need to unburden or collect yourself and then come to Jesus. Your very burden is what qualifies you to come. No payment is required. He says, "I will give you rest." His rest is gift, not transaction. Whether you are actively working hard to crowbar

your life into smoothness ("labor") or passively finding your-self weighed down by something outside your control ("heavy laden"), Jesus Christ's desire that you find rest, that you come in out of the storm, outstrips even your own.[3]

This is the invitation of Matthew 11:28–30: That as we get away with God, as we enter into oneness with Him, we will recover our lives. That as we actually lose our lives, we will gain them. As we seek Him, we will find joy and peace and love. To "learn the unforced rhythms of grace." And this grace is not earned by our own efforts or accomplishments, but rather it is a gift. Freely given. Our only job is to receive it.

I know you're weary, exhausted. Your journey may be treach-erous right now. It may feel like it's all too much. Or that you're too much.

You may feel weighed down by the heaviness of life. You've been carrying that burden for far too long.

COME.

Jesus is inviting you to come.

He is longing to sit with you and teach you a new way. A way of peace and rest and full life. To show you how to live lightly and freely. He wants to breathe life into your weariness, to hold you up in your exhaustion, and to give you a burden that is light. Oh, there's a burden to bear, but in Him, it is easy because you are not responsible for the outcome.

One way *rest* in Matthew 11:28–30 can be defined is "to keep quiet, of calm and patient expectation."[4] This verse is an invitation to come to Jesus and learn how to walk with Him, and He gives a promise that is repeated twice: You will find rest for your soul, the most important thing about you, your inner being. And the rest that He gives, it flows from all that is within Him.

Jesus longs to offer you Himself, and within the depth of who He is, He gives you refreshment and joy.

This book is an invitation to draw nearer to God and learn how to walk with Him and hear His voice, despite the loud voices that woo us away from His peace and taunt us. How do we find rest from the exhaustion of life? How do we learn to truly trust Jesus with the heavy things that are out of our control, past our managing? How do we become women who are secure in our true identities, while still being vulnerable and able to take risks? How do we stay softhearted through all the pain that tempts us to harden our hearts?

Come, Jesus says, all who are weary. Will you come?

Spiritual Practice

Rest for your weary soul comes as you get away with Jesus. Sit and take a big breath. Let yourself get into your body. Then open your hands and recite Psalm 23 to the Lord. Ask Him to be your Shepherd and to show you how to walk in His ways, to lead you beside still waters and green pastures. Imagine still waters and green pastures in your mind. What does it feel like to be there? What does it smell like? What do you see?

Think about whether there is anything that is weighing you down right now and give that to the Lord. Ask Him to take the burden from you and to show you how to walk in the unforced rhythms of grace.

QUIZ: HOW EXHAUSTED ARE YOU?

Does your soul feel weary and exhausted? Have you been carrying a heavy burden? Take this quiz to see where you are on the spectrum of exhaustion.

For each question, rate yourself on a scale of 0 to 5, 0 being not at all, 5 being yes, always. At the end, add the numbers up to determine if you are living with exhaustion in your life.

____ I feel defeated when things go wrong even though I worked really hard to ensure I covered all my bases.

____ I feel hopeless when what I say or do doesn't change the situation or the person.

____ I feel like I'm floating and can't get grounded.

____ I feel like people are just getting pieces of me.

____ I wonder how much longer this will go on.

____ I feel like it's all up to me and I am alone.

____ I feel like I'm at the end of my rope, at a total loss as to what to do next.

____ I feel like I did all the things I could, and I'm still waiting.

____ I feel bone weary and have a hard time facing another day.

____ I am having emotional meltdowns and can't seem to regulate.

____ My chest feels heavy often, making it hard to take deep breaths.

____ I feel stuck in my thoughts, trying to find solutions or wondering where it went wrong, but can't get out of the loop.

____ I'm afraid of doing something or saying something that will set that person off.

____ I feel like I'm a slave to my to-do list.

____ I go to bed at night feeling defeated and insecure.

____ I feel behind.

____ I go to Google seeking answers to my problems before I go to the Lord or others.

____ I have a hard time falling asleep, or staying asleep, because of all that is weighing on my mind.

____ I don't know what to do with my disappointments.

____ I don't know what to do with my hurt and longings, so I just try to set them aside.

____ It feels too scary or overwhelming to face the hard things in my inner life.

If you scored 60 or more, you may be living from a place of exhaustion because you are trying to manage the outcomes and neglecting your heart in the process. Perhaps you feel like you're coming undone with all that is hard in your life.

If you scored 40 or more, you may be weary and needing God's presence to comfort you and fill you with hope in the depths of your heart.

If you scored 30 or more, you may be tired and needing some deep refreshment for your soul.

Wherever you landed on this quiz, I'm excited to journey together with you in discovering how to live from a place of rest and restore your soul. Let's discover what God longs for you and how to become a person of deep love, peace, and joy as you learn to walk with Him, in His way, with His presence.

2

HEART MATTERS

I was sitting on the front porch on a mid-July day. The sun was shining above me, the birds were singing around me, the ever-so-slight breeze was keeping me cool. It was a gorgeous day. Peaceful, calm. And yet the interior of my heart was not at peace. In fact, I would likely have cried at the drop of a hat with just the right word or question. I was angsty, discontent, and stressed. Even a beautiful day like that couldn't bring the peace that I longed for.

I was talking to Jeff, my husband, who squinted up at me, attempting to block the sun from his eyes.

I could tell he was trying to understand me, trying to sympathize and patiently listen. But the truth was, I was all over the map. He couldn't offer me the peace I was longing for, and I wasn't quite at the place to receive help. I needed to process, to release this pressure inside of me, but it felt like even as I tried to do that, I still felt overwhelmed, exhausted, and fragmented.

We had just moved into our new home, which we had purchased six months before. It was up on the mountain, overlooking Maui's north shore, with lemon and orange and lime trees surrounding the house. It was a dream and had been a total answer to prayer. Although the house was grand, it hadn't been our style, with lots of dark rock and yellow walls and dated bathrooms, and it had been abandoned for six years, so the rats had made their home there. The roof was leaking, and honeybees had infested one of the rooms, so much so that honey would drip from the ceiling and the windows were covered with thousands of bees. Our friend who is a contractor from California moved into this rat-infested house with his family (bless them) and had been remodeling it for the past six months. Jeff would go up to the house every day as well, to help demo and put in new floors and do carpentry work.

Prior to the move, we had lived an hour away from our new home, and having Jeff gone every day was new for us, since he'd been working from home our whole marriage. It had been six months of long hours, long weeks, and me at home with three littles with no car for months; not to mention the stress of remodeling! I was lonely. There were so many decisions, and if you know my husband, you know he moves fast. We would joke that every decision had to be made in sixty seconds. (It was mostly true.) And as with all remodeling jobs, the timeframe tripled, the budget tripled, and the stress tripled. This was all on top of our already busy everyday lives.

So there we were, finally moved into our home, all the contractors gone, and we were trying to learn a new rhythm of life. A new community. A new location. I had thought since we were still on the same island, it wouldn't be that much different from our old life, but I was proven wrong. Even a move an hour away can turn your whole world upside down.

Although remodeled and freshly painted, the house still had rooms that needed work. The HVAC system still needed to be updated, and incredibly ugly orange carpet needed to be ripped out. But we were fresh out of cash. So I was trying to learn to be thankful and content and live in imperfection and wait for change down the road, but it was proving to be more challenging than I thought to live with loose ends. To not have the time in the day to do all the things I wanted to accomplish, or to not be able to finish things as I liked. There were no checking things off this list! I was so grateful for our home, but it wasn't where I thought it would be at this point.

But it wasn't just the house. It was my heart that didn't seem right.

It felt run ragged. It was as if we had run ninety miles per hour nonstop for the last six months, and now that we could rest, I didn't know how. And when I finally slowed down, I realized that I wasn't okay. All the things that I had pushed aside, all that I had told myself would be fine once we moved, all that I had buried or pushed down was now coming to the surface, and I didn't know what to do with it.

I felt burned-out. Anxious.

I felt like I didn't even know where to begin to recover.

Because it wasn't just the house and the move; it was our family too. Jeff and I had divided and conquered and let it go on for too long. The kids were adjusting to a new normal and were going through some big emotional leaps that I wasn't sure how to navigate. And I was so disconnected from my own self. I had been surviving, doing, always on to the next thing, and although I deeply loved Jesus and talked with Him every day, I felt like my faith and my everyday life were having a hard time being unified. It was as if I'd read my Bible in the morning and then forget about it for the rest of the day. It wasn't infiltrating my life and transforming me as I had hoped. I was so busy doing things for God but not learning to live in His presence.

I had also been trying to hold together our family along with caring for everyone's needs; I felt like it was my job to ensure that they were doing well emotionally. Sometimes I felt like I was walking on eggshells, trying to make sure none of my kids got upset about anything.

I just can't handle that today, I'd think.

If someone in our family was sad, I felt like I had to cheer them up.

If someone was angry, I felt like I had to calm them down.

Life was chaotic and turned upside down, but the reality was that my inner being was chaotic and turned upside down.

I was starting to crumble. All the things I had pushed aside, stuffed down, were now coming out sideways, and I was combusting.

The remodel was stressful for Jeff too. Toward the end of the project, he was more stressed out than I'd seen him before. I wanted to help and care for him, but I wasn't sure how. I wanted to share my feelings and thoughts with him, but I didn't always know how or when, and truth be told, I thought I could just sweep them under the rug. *I don't want to lay that on him on top of everything else,* I'd think. Or often when I did try to share, it all came out wrong. As I tried to keep things in, my heart started to grow cold. Critical thoughts, bitterness, and burdens weighed me down.

I thought I was caring for my family's hearts, but really, I was trying to manage their circumstances so they could be happy. So I could be at peace.

But really, it was a false peace that didn't give me the promise I was hoping for.

Little did I know that that conversation with Jeff on the porch that day would be the beginning of a new way of learning the unforced rhythms of grace for me. Not because of any revelation I had or anything amazing Jeff said to me (although he often gives such great insight), but because for the first time I was letting out what I had buried and stuffed down for so long, and it was ugly. I didn't like it. I couldn't fix it. And I realized that it was starting to spill out onto others.

I understood that I needed change. I needed to go there. I needed to stop neglecting my heart and to open it up. To God, to others whom I trusted to speak into my life. I needed to slow down and tend to my heart instead of trying to manage everyone else's.

This was the beginning of my journey of learning to truly walk with God, to hear His voice, and to grow in closer unity with Him. And it wasn't because of a five-step process or a formula I followed. But rather, it began with my heart. God was inviting me to come to Him as I was, right where I was—with a heart that was heavy and overwhelmed.

This quote, often attributed to Dallas Willard, says, "If you don't come away for a while, you'll come apart after a while."

God was inviting me to come away with Him—not on a retreat or a vacation (although that would have been divine!) but to come away with Him throughout my days, to turn my eyes toward Him, and to give Him my heart, in real-time, true honesty. We are called to come while we are heavy laden. This was an invitation to the practice of silence and solitude in my everyday life.

A few months later, my friend Sara sent me three books for my birthday. One of them was John Eldredge's book *Waking the Dead: The Secret to a Heart Fully Alive*.[1] In the package, she wrote a little note saying that these books were some of her favorites and she thought I would enjoy them as well.

It felt like a hug. Because, well, for starters, books are my love language. My dream day would include lying by the pool at the beach for eight hours reading, with some poolside-service guacamole and a piña colada. (Perhaps you are reading this right now doing the same thing, and if so, we would be best friends.)

Slightly teary, I hugged the books close, feeling seen and known.

What did I need?

I desperately needed my heart to come back to life. Was that possible? What did that look like in my thirties? This is the time in your life when you are more passionate than ever before about specific things and yet have more responsibility than ever before. The time in your life when you still dream, but you have experienced the realities that come with each dream. You know what you're signing up for now. You know the cost. It's the time in your life when you maybe did all the right things, and yet the life you thought had been promised to you doesn't look like you thought it would. Or you do have the life you always dreamed of, but it's a lot harder than you ever imagined. Pain, suffering, trials are ever more present in your life and in the lives of those around you. Disillusionment comes into full swing in your thirties. Your ideals are met with reality, and you don't know what to do with it all.

I read and reread that John Eldredge book and highlighted and underlined it in a way where you would have thought the book was twenty years old. It was like water to my weary soul. It gave me permission to go there. To take the time, to make it a priority to tend to my heart, to bring it before God, to be curious with myself, to haul up all that had been pushed down, and to look at myself with gentleness and kindness in Jesus' presence.

That day on the porch with Jeff was the beginning of my heart coming back to life, not because my problems were solved or my stress dissipated or my outcomes changed, but rather because it revealed to me that I needed help. I couldn't go on like that anymore. I was coming undone. I was falling apart. Not my outward life per se, although it certainly wasn't perfect. But rather, my inner life. My soul was not okay. I was weary, run ragged, unable to wrap things up in a tidy bow. I could not stop my unraveling, and my unraveling was impacting my family. I was not the most steady or loving wife; I was not the most steady or loving mom. I couldn't keep it all together anymore. And for the first time in my life, I was accepting the gift of becoming undone instead of running from it. It was the very fact that I was unraveling that I could run to the Father to be put back together not just to survive, but to be a whole and holy person.

For so long I had followed Jesus and loved the Bible (I mean, I cry thinking about the gift of God's Word) and knew verses for so many areas of my life, but I didn't know how to bring my true self to God. I didn't know how to have His words fully impact my heart, because I didn't bring my full heart to Him. How could He touch the places in me that were becoming fragmented and falling apart if I didn't bring them to Him? Augustine wrote in Confessions, in AD 400, "How can you draw close to God when you are far from your own self?" He prayed: "Grant, Lord, that I may know myself that I may know thee."[2]

We know God, but are we known by Him? Do we know ourselves? Are we self-aware? And do we bring our true selves to God? We can only know God as much as we are known and know ourselves.

I had thought my heart didn't matter so much. Oh, I knew He loved me and cared for me and delighted in me, but I didn't know how deeply He cared for my heart and longed to know it with no judgment. I thought I had to show up in a certain way. I didn't fully know His tenderness, His gentleness, His deep care.

God is after our hearts more than our accomplishments.

Somehow, I had come to believe that I needed to do good things for Him to earn His love. Yes, He wants to partner with us and He asks us to serve, but it's the fruit of our relationship with Jesus, not the basis of it. The problem comes when we disassociate from our hearts and try to earn our hearts through what we can achieve.

God cares more about your heart than anything you'll ever do, or what will be said of you, or what will be written about you. He cares more for your heart than the income you make, the promotions you get, the goals you set. He cares more for your heart than what you can check off your list, show on Instagram, get done in a week, or put on your resume.

He wants you. Not what you can do for Him. But you. Your heart, mind, body, and spirit. He wants your whole self, fully open, surrendered, and willing to receive from Him.

That is the most important.

The calling, the assignments, the life seasons—that all comes after. Yes, God created us to partner together with Him to defeat darkness and share His light and love with the world. That is our purpose in life. But before we say yes to that, we must sit with Him and learn what it means to be His child.

Now, what does it mean when I say God cares most for your heart? What is the heart?

When I was in college, my best friend, Kaelyn, would always look me in the eyes with such sincerity and ask me, "How's your heart, Lyss?"

Back then I had such a hard time opening up. Letting people in to know and understand my heart was hard. I wanted to so badly, but I was so afraid. So I'd always wait until the conversation was almost done and finally spill. But Kaelyn was the one who taught me to be vulnerable. Nothing would surprise her. She never tried to fix my problems right away. She was curious. She listened. She empathized. She created a safe place for me to feel like I could be totally honest and not judged. Totally honest and fully loved. And she'd still always point me to Jesus and sharpen me.

So ever since then, I've always asked the people in my life, "How's your heart?"

But it wasn't until that summer that I started to ask myself that question. And not with judgment, but with curiosity. And then I would go move my body—go for a walk—and think about it. And talk to God about it.

How's my heart, Lyss?

Geri Scazzero says this in *The Emotionally Healthy Woman*:

Failing to acknowledge what is going on in your heart eventually results in losing connection with yourself. And if you lose connection with yourself, you easily slip out of dependency on God's Spirit…knowing your heart requires standing in God's presence and asking yourself some difficult questions about your actions, reactions, motives, feelings, and thoughts.[3]

We have to ask ourselves then, what is the heart?

Dane Ortlund, in his book *Gentle and Lowly*, says this about the heart:

When the Bible speaks of the heart, whether Old Testament or New, it is not speaking of our emotional life only but of the central animating center of all we do. It is what gets us out of bed in the morning and what we daydream about as we drift off to sleep. It is our motivation headquarters. The heart, in biblical terms, is not part of who we are but the center of who we are. Our heart is what defines and directs us.[4]

King Solomon said in Proverbs 4:23, "Keep your heart with all vigilance, for from it flow the springs of life."

Our heart is core to who we are. It is the center of our being. Everything flows from our heart. In America, we often believe that the heart is equal to our emotions. So we say, *Follow your heart, and go with your feelings, and let those lead you.* This is terrible advice. Yes, emotions are part of our heart, but our heart also includes our mind. It's our emotions and our mind. Our feelings and our thoughts. It is where we hold our deepest allegiances and values. Our thoughts and emotions go hand in hand. When we think something, there is always a feeling to go with it. And when we feel something, there is always a thought behind it.

If our heart is core to who we are, then why do we neglect it? Why do we not tend to it? Why do we try to numb it, or push it under the rug, or treat it with shame? Or why do we not nourish it with all that is good and lovely? If it is the wellspring of life, as King Solomon (the wisest man on earth) said, why do we shut it down or let it leak all over? Moses says in Deuteronomy 6:4–6, "Hear, O Israel: The LORD our God, the LORD is one. You shall love the LORD your God with all your heart and with all your soul and with all your might. And these words that I command you today shall be on your heart."

We are called to love God with all of our hearts. Our full selves. Everything within us. This is fullness of life. God wants to give us all of Himself, so we can be full of Him and love Him with all of who we are. But how can He give us all of Himself if we do not open up all of ourselves to Him?

Think of it like our abs, our "core." My friend recently had a tummy tuck to strengthen her muscles and put them back together after having five children. She had no idea how brutal the surgery was going to be. For weeks, she couldn't bend over to put on socks, or sit up without help to drink water. Her core had been torn apart to be put back together, and it was going to take a long time to heal and restrengthen those muscles. Our "core" really does hold up and help us to do all the things.

The heart is the will or spirit of a person. It is what gives us the "power to do what is good—or evil"[5] and lies at the very center of who we are. Our lives are not run by the heart alone (but it is the place we look at first, before God).

Now, the world will say, *Follow your heart. Do what makes you happy. Do what feels best.*

The world tells us that our feelings should lead us, that our feelings should be at the core of all we say and do. The world's formula is, *If you feel something, do it. If you feel like something, you are something.*

However, feelings are not meant to lead us. They give us important information about our body and our needs. They're meant to lead us to investigate what is in our hearts, so we can bring it to the surface and find healing and freedom and help. Sure, feelings often come upon us like a rush of wind, and we feel powerless under them, but we need to be curious as to what they're communicating, whether our needs are being met, and then act accordingly. My friend Tristen Collins is a trauma therapist who gives this great framework for understanding our emotions:

Three *N*s:

1. Notice—acknowledge what is happening in your body (*Do I feel hot? Is my chest or back tight or numb?*).
2. Name—interpret your body's sensations as a specific feeling (*I am feeling anxious, angry, discouraged*).

3. Navigate—explore what you need and the different strategies to meet those needs.

She encourages us to be curious and open to different ways of meeting the needs that are revealed, as they won't always be the same. For instance, if I am feeling angry, like I'm going to explode, maybe I need to go for a walk today, while other times I may need to go hit some balls on the pickleball court.

Emotions are gifts from God to show us what is going on in our hearts so we can live in healthy relationships and be united with Him.

The heart is our central station, where good and evil can come from (Mark 7:21). The goal in the Christian life is not to change our behaviors, but to be transformed into the likeness of God for the glory of God, which all starts in the heart.

God gives us a new heart when we give our lives to Him. We give Him our heart of stone, and He gives us a heart of flesh (Ezek. 11:19). And God will be found when we seek Him with all of our heart (Jer. 29:13).

Clearly, the heart is important—vital, in fact. And it is the heart that needs transformation. When we seek God with our whole heart, and He transforms us through the power of the Holy Spirit, we then change our whole selves.

Your heart matters.

It is what connects you to God. Connects you to others. It's what makes you fully alive.

And that's exactly why the enemy longs to distract and discourage you. It's why he causes you to neglect and try to earn your heart and why you often lose heart. He wants to make you asleep, small, and insignificant. Because a heart fully alive in Jesus is powerful and changes the atmosphere.

Months after I had received those books from my friend Sara, I was walking along the hill by our house that is lined with eucalyptus trees, listening to a vox that she sent. She was responding to one I had sent the week before in which I told her how I felt like I was unraveling. Every week I'd inevitably have one major breakdown. Midday, I'd end up in my bedroom, weeping on the floor. Although I had been learning about my heart coming back to life, and longing for it to be made alive again, I was face-to-face with a lot of hard in my home.

I remember her message as clear as day. She said to me, "Lyss, I think you should take time to tend to your heart. Whatever it takes. It might be two months; it might be a year. If you need to let things slide for a while, that's okay. Your kids will be okay. The most important thing is that you are doing well so you can pour out from a full cup. Ask Jeff to help. Say no. Make firm boundaries. You need the time and space to be, and to process, and to care for your heart."

Not that I needed permission, but it gave me permission. (Funny how that works sometimes.) She was saying it was not only okay but vital for me to tend to my heart.

In our culture today, this could be understood as "self-care": *Do whatever it takes to make sure you're happy. Go get that manicure! Go buy that dress! You first.*

That's not what I'm talking about here. (Although I do love a good manicure and a fun new dress!)

I'm talking about soul care. How can we care for the thing that is most important? How do we make it a priority to mark out time to get away and be? Not do. To be curious with ourselves. To be self-aware of all that is stirring in our hearts so we can connect to the heart of God?

Often, we live our days all tangled up inside. We have encounters with people that leave us floundering a bit, or hurt, or frustrated. We wake up to days that bring chaos and disorder and stress. We experience unwanted moments, unwanted encounters, unwanted thoughts and feelings.

But instead of being gracious with ourselves, being soft and curious, we rush on ahead, focused on the next task, not giving ourselves the time or space to get untangled—sometimes because we're afraid of going there, unsure of what will arise, unsure of whether it'll just leave us spinning out of control more and unable to get through the day. Or we simply don't value our hearts. We think we are what we do, what we can accomplish, our performance, so what does it matter what we feel about something or why that affected us so much? We need to just keep going.

But God invites us to get away with Him and open up our hearts to Him. To get untangled so we don't unravel. He invites us to a posture of curiosity, patience, kindness.

I think sometimes we think God is sitting there as our judge, with His arms crossed and looking stern, ready to correct us and tell us all that we're doing wrong. This is not who God is! Yes, He is a judge and will bring justice (praise God! I'm so thankful we serve a God who does what is right, who is true, who protects the poor and cares for the vulnerable and will bring justice on evil). But He does not sit arms crossed and stern. He sits with arms stretched out, hands open, with gentleness in His eyes and an invitation on His face to come. He longs to care for you, to know you, to bring healing and grace and freedom. It's His kindness that leads us to repentance (Romans 2:4). His love that transforms.

And so in His presence, we can stop and ask ourselves, *When this happened yesterday, what was I feeling? What was underlying that feeling? Did someone say something? Did it trigger something in me? What was I thinking? What was I believing?*

And then we can go further. Thinking about what has us all twisted up, we can ask, *Is that God's heart for me? Is that a lie? Is it true?*

Whatever we uncover, we can then talk to God about it. Confess where we are wrong. Confess where we are believing lies. And choose to replace those lies with what He says in His Word, what is true.

When my friend gave me permission to tend to my heart, that was the beginning of my journey of learning new spiritual disciplines that invited me into the heart of God. It slowed my pace down, and as I did it, I felt more and more human. More and more whole. More and more alive.

The biggest game changer for me was going for an afternoon walk every day. As I walked, I would ask myself these two questions:

1. *Where have I seen and felt God's presence today?*

2. *Where have I not seen or felt God's presence today?*

And sure enough, every afternoon as I walked that hill, I would gain a new perspective. God was with me. God was present. I just needed to open my eyes to see it.

The areas where I didn't see His presence—often, the areas in which I was frustrated or sad or mad—were usually revealed to be the places where I was believing a lie. Whenever I realized that, I would take a moment and confess to the Lord and receive His love.

Your heart is important. It matters. And it's worth it to do whatever you can to tend to it. Becoming self-aware of what is going on in your heart is key to finding freedom from the heavy burdens of life. It all starts with noticing what you are holding inside of you and then bringing it before God.

Spiritual Practice

Sit with journal open for a few moments and ask yourself if anything feels all tangled up inside of you right now.

And then, as my friend Diane Comer has taught me, askhese two questions:

1. What is that about? (Be curious; be kind with yourself. The purpose is to discover and give space for you to realize why you feel tangled up in that way, over that situation. You don't need to fix it. Just ask what's going on.)
2. Ask the Lord, "What do you want me to do about it?" This is a beautiful prayer, as sometimes you will be surprised at what God reveals. Sometimes, there will be actions for you to do; sometimes it will look like confession or changing your mind or placing that burden into His hands. Sometimes it will look like doing something practically. Either way, I promise it will unburden you and be so much more kind than you would expect.

Spend a few moments giving thanks for where you do see God at work in your life and take time to talk to God about the area(s) you don't. Be curious. Confess. Ask Him for what is true and take note of that.

3

DESIRES

Longing is the heart's treasury.   —AUGUSTINE

One of the swiftest ways to awaken your heart, and to connect with the heart of God, is to think about what you desire. What do you want? What are you longing for?

David Benner, psychologist, professor, and author, says, "For what we long for in our heart we will pursue with the totality of our being—not simply with the resolve of our will."[1]

A few months ago, I visited one of my mentors, Tammy, at her beautiful hacienda in California. She made us coffee with the most delicious and luscious foamed cream, and we walked up the hill in her backyard and sat down in two comfy chairs. An olive tree hung over us, birds were singing around us, and as we talked, we overlooked all of downtown Anaheim. It was a gorgeous California day. Dry. Warm. The sun on my face. Coffee in hand. Friend by my side.

We quickly got to the "good stuff"—the deep, heart-to-heart matters. And as I shared how I was doing, what was happening, I had a really hard time understanding how my heart actually was doing. Tammy helped me name my pain points and encouraged me with deep truth. Then, ever so simply, she looked at me and asked, "Alyssa, what do you want?"

I opened my mouth, but nothing came out. I stopped. I stuttered. I closed my mouth.

What do I want?

Gosh, I hadn't really thought about that in so long. I had been busy considering everyone else and had once again lost touch with my own heart.

As women, we are told to do all the things, be all the things, all right now. Nothing can hold us back! Go for it!

As Nike famously proclaims, "Just do it!"

We see everyone's lives on display with a tap of the finger, and it's hard to not come away feeling like we need to do that or be that too. And sometimes it's not even comparison, but rather this desire to excel, to know it all, to be the best—whether for us or for our families.

I want to be toxin-free.

I want to eat healthy.

I want to move my body.

I want to dress cute.

I want to have an organized home.

I want to see the world.

I want to learn.

I want to make memories.

I want to make my life beautiful, my home beautiful, myself beautiful.

I want to look young.

I want to be knowledgeable and wise.

I want to leave a legacy.

I want to be intentional as a parent.

I want to be a good wife.

I want to have fun.

I want to change the world.

I want to be financially stable.

I want to have a fulfilling career.

I want a goldendoodle.

I want to go to the Taylor Swift concert! (It's like a rite of passage as a woman to go!)

And I want all those things within a matter of ten minutes.

The thing is, we are living in a time where we have more opportunity than ever before, and our culture revels in that. What freedom! However, with so much opportunity, for women especially, there are expectations—like the expectation that not only can we want all of it, but we *should* go for it all. We should do it all, and we should be able to do it all well.

These are all good things, good desires. We were created to have desires, to long, to want. It's how we're wired.

Our desires are, in fact, what draw us to God.

They're also what draw us away.

When God created the world in Genesis 1–2, it was beautiful and full of peace and rest and delight because God was with humankind and walked among them. In Hebrew, this is called shalom. Theologian Cornelius Plantinga describes *shalom* like this:

> The webbing together of God, humans, and all creation in justice, fulfillment, and delight is what the Hebrew prophets call shalom. We call it peace, but it means far more than mere peace of mind or a cease-fire between enemies. In the Bible, shalom means universal flourishing, wholeness, and delight—a rich state of affairs in which natural needs are satisfied and natural gifts fruitfully employed, a state of affairs that inspires joyful wonder as its

Creator and Savior opens doors and welcomes the creatures in whom he delights. Shalom, in other words, is the way things ought to be.[2]

Ecclesiastes 3:11 says that God "has put eternity into man's heart."

From the very beginning, we long for eternity. We long for shalom. For flourishing lives, flourishing families, flourishing communities and cities. For all that is broken to be made whole. For wrongs to be made right. For hurts to be healed, lives to be made holy. We long for what ought to be.

At our core, we long to be loved, to be seen, to be known, to be secure, to be cared for.

I also believe we long to live a life full of purpose. A life full of meaning, one that impacts others for good.

In Genesis 1–2, the Bible beautifully, poetically describes the Lord creating the world and all that's in it. The moon, sun, land, sea, birds, fish, animals, and as the culmination of creation, humankind.

And all of this, He says, is good. It is very good.

You see, from the very beginning, there was a war going on. Satan had wanted to be worshipped too, and full of pride, he went against God, and a full-on war began. Good versus evil. God versus Satan.

Genesis 1:1–2 says, "In the beginning, God created the heavens and the earth. The earth was without form and void, and darkness was over the face of the deep. And the Spirit of God was hovering over the face of the waters." *Without form and void* here means it was uncultivated and uninhabited. It needed to be filled and organized. It was chaos. *The deep* to the Jews in ancient times was a place of chaos and mess and was often portrayed as evil. It was not like the peaceful waters of Maui that people love to go surfing in! This is war language. And within these two verses, within this war context of when the earth was created, God situates Himself between it. He creates, and His Spirit is present.

God had created something so good and put humans there to cultivate it and organize it and create goodness from it. It was not perfect, because it was not complete. There was work yet to be done. However, it was full of shalom because God was there.

As my beloved seminary professor Gerry Breshears says, God created humankind in His own image to partner with Him in defeating darkness. How do we defeat darkness? With light. We overcome the uninhabited by being fruitful and multiplying, by discipleship. We seek His face, and as we're transformed into His likeness, we are made to disciple others to do the same. We are made to create other image bearers to bring goodness, justice, peace, and beauty to their communities, to then create communities that bring goodness, justice, and beauty to their cities.

So not only are we made with deep desires to be loved, we also are made with an innate desire to make places of shalom.

We long for what ought to be. Pastor and author John Mark Comer talks about our desires for shalom in our inner being by explaining how "our strongest desires are not actually our deepest desires."[3]

Our strong desires are what we want now. What we desire here and now. These things can be good and valid. We need to take note of those desires, to consider them, because they show us what's going on in our heart.

The list of my desires on pages 35 and 36 are my strong desires. In any given moment, any given day. They can bombard me and swarm my soul. Right now, as I sit in my chair, I would love a pedicure (because I'm looking at my half-chipped nail polish); a phone date with my best friend, Emilie; and a really good laugh, the kind that makes you cry and your abs hurt.

Those are my "midland" desires. They are more what's on the surface. But if I looked a little closer I'd probably see that I am desiring those because I feel weary. I'm tired and I'm a little lonely. I need friendship, and I need care.

Those things bring joy to my life, they spark a little something in me, but I can't look to a pedicure or even one of my best friends to fill me. They are gifts. But I need to go to God first and seek Him to care for my weary and lonely soul.

Often our strong desires are not our deepest desires. They are the first ones we go to, the easiest to face. And they are where we operate most of our lives from. But beneath those desires are much deeper ones that God has given us.

Comer says, "Underneath all of the other desires that people are often living off of and out of is this deep primal desire to be with God and to become deeply formed into a person of love."[4]

As believers with regenerated hearts, we have deep, beautiful desires. They hit the deep places of our heart. Our longings, hopes, dreams. But often, because life is so busy or painful, we don't go to our deepest desires. Instead, we operate out of our strongest desires, the desires of the flesh, the ones that seem more in-our-face, more urgent, more tangible and that tempt us into believing they are more fulfilling and are often easier to deal with than our deep desires.

Going to my example of a good pedicure and a good call with my best friend, yes—I feel lonely and weary. But my deepest desire? What I'm really desperate for? It's to connect with the heart of God in a way that refreshes my soul. I'm really longing for Him. I need His encouragement, His relief and peace, and His love. I long to be a good friend, I long to bless and pour out to others, but I can only do that as I spend time with Jesus and have Him pour into me.

Strong desire. Deep desire. Deepest desire.

Desire is important, but there are two problems with it. First is what John Eldredge calls the "desire dilemma," which is when we desire something but don't get it. It's painful, sometimes unbearably so. He says, "Is this not the source of nearly all our pain and sorrow?"[5]

We grow up having dreams and desires galore. Childlike faith, utter joy. But then reality hits. We face pain, hurt, rejection, shame, disappointment, and despair. We hoped for something, we desired it, we asked God for it, and it didn't happen. Or it did but ended in utter failure. It was so much worse than we could have ever imagined. So much more painful. Or it simply wasn't what we thought it would be; it let us down. Desire is risking and being vulnerable, and once we've been let down, we often hesitate to go there in our hearts again. To be let down again. To be hurt again. Often, we can close that part of our hearts off. We can numb the desires, settle, or become apathetic. We start to just get by. We close off our hearts from wanting, from hoping, because our expectations weren't met, our ideals did not come to fruition.

This is as good as it gets.

This will do.

I don't want to get my hopes up.

I just want to be prepared for the worst, or if it doesn't happen.

John Eldredge says,

We abandon the most important journey of our lives when we abandon desire. We leave our hearts by the side of the road and head off in the direction of fitting in, getting by, being productive, what have you. Whatever we might gain—money, position, the approval of others, or just absence of the discontent itself—it's not worth it. "What good will it be for a man if he gains the whole world, yet forfeits his soul?" (Matt. 16:26).[6]

The second problem is disordered desires. Disordered desires are when we desire things or people more than God; this is known as idolatry. We become attached to them, thinking they'll provide and give us the love, meaning, delight, peace that we are looking for. We are made to attach and to be loved—that's why it's so important for babies in their first two years to have someone that they can depend on to love and care for them. We are made to attach to God.

So often we look to other people and other things to satisfy us. We look to marriage to be the thing that will make us feel loved and cared for and never alone. We look to children to give us meaning and joy. We look to money for comfort. We look to success to validate our value and worth. We look to beauty products to make us feel beautiful and worthy to be seen. We look to books or Google to give us knowledge so we can have a place at the table to talk and be seen as someone worth being listened to.

Our desires can be good.

And they can be easily disordered.

After God created the heavens and the earth and all the things to fill it and said that it was very good, He also told Adam and Eve that they could eat from any of the trees in the garden, except for one—the tree of the knowledge of good and evil. They could have their pick, but one tree He didn't want them to eat from. Why? Because He wanted them to stay attached to Him. He wanted them to trust Him for wisdom and guidance and communion. He knew that when they ate from that tree, their fellowship would be broken. Sin would enter the world. Shame would make its home.

So Satan comes on the scene as a sneaky snake and questions Eve.

Did God really say…?

Eve misquotes God by saying not only could they not eat from it, but they also couldn't touch it. She makes Him to be stricter than He was, although she fully understood His command.

Satan then blatantly lies to her: "You will not surely die. For God knows that when you eat of it your eyes will be opened, and you will be like God, knowing good and evil" (Gen. 3:4–5).

You will be like God. You will get to define what is good or bad by yourself; you don't need to rely on God or anyone else. Independence is the goal.

This is the exact opposite of God's purpose and God's heart. He longs for us to be dependent on Him, to live in intimacy with Him, not apart.

But Eve wanted to do it her way; she wanted to judge for herself what was best, instead of relying on God's wisdom and submitting to His command.

> So when the woman saw that the tree was good for food, and that it was a delight to the eyes, and that the tree was to be desired to make one wise, she took of its fruit and ate, and she also gave some to her husband who was with her, and he ate. (Genesis 3:6)

Eve took matters into her own hands. We don't know her motives here, but I can see how she could have been doubting God's goodness to her and thinking He was withholding good from her. She trusted herself more than God because it was safer. She saw that the fruit was good, and it was a delight, and she desired it. She wanted it. So she ate it, not trusting in God.

Eve desired to be Christlike—a good desire. But that desire can quickly become distorted by wanting to be God. We want to control our lives, to make the calls, to define what is good on our own.

Instead of trusting God and His wisdom, Eve wanted to be wise without God and do what she thought was best.

And so, sin entered the world.

And the curse.

And the promise for redemption.

And throughout this whole story, God comes. He pursues.

Where are you?

He doesn't shame Adam and Eve. He doesn't scold them. He doesn't give up on them. But He comes looking for them, asking questions. Drawing them out. His heart grieved over their sin, and even in the breaking, He promised a way for full restoration in Jesus.

Eve desired. But it became distorted. She attached herself to the fruit instead of God Himself.

David Benner gives great insight into discerning between disordered desires and pure desires. He says, "Ordered, or purified, desires expand me and connect me to others and the world in life-enhancing ways. Disordered desires suck me into myself and rather than adding vitality to life, leach it away. This is because ordered desires spring from willingness and surrender, while disordered ones are my willful attempt to arrange for my own happiness and fulfillment."[7]

I am a peacemaker. I don't like conflict, and when I say I don't like it, I mean I run from it. Avoid it at all costs. Push it down. Pretend it's not there, although it's all I think about. At least, I used to. I'm learning to step into the uncomfortable and have the hard conversations these days.

A few years ago, I had one of my first counseling sessions. My counselor is amazing, and you'll hear me quote him quite a bit in this book because he's been so instrumental in my formation. This day, I was sitting in Jeff's office, early in the morning over Zoom, trying to describe to my counselor my problem. I had this relationship where I was scared to ever bring up anything that hurt me, or to address things that needed to change. In my heart, I was desiring peace. I didn't want conflict. I wanted this person to like me and be pleased with me, and I never wanted to ruffle any feathers.

He looked at me with his fatherly, tender eyes, and said, "It sounds to me like what you really are longing for is intimacy, but you're settling for a false peace."

Silence. Oof.

For so many years, I had been trying to keep the peace, thinking that's what I wanted most, that that was what was most important, when really, I wanted intimacy. I wanted to be close. To be vulnerable. To be known and loved. And although I thought that's what we had because I wasn't bringing up conflict to break that intimacy, I really wasn't being known and I didn't have peace either.

Strong desire versus deep desire.

Intimacy takes work. It's harder. It's way more vulnerable. But it's worth it. It's honest. It's real. It's good. It's my deepest desire.

Eldredge says, "Desire, both the whispers and the shouts, is the map we have been given to find the only life worth living."[8]

We must take note of what we desire, but even more important is learning to long for the sacred. Not just the good, but the holy. To hunger and thirst for God, and for the things of God. What would happen if God's people started to long for Jesus? To long for people to know Jesus? To long for not just a good life, but a life that is consecrated, committed, sold-out for God?

To know, deep to our cores, that we are His and He is ours and to give our lives away for His kingdom to take up more space here on earth?

What if we longed for God to increase in us?

Increase our capacity for You, God. Increase our capacity to do all that You long to do in Your heart.

I think the world, our worlds, would be radically different. Full of light. Full of purpose. Full of power.

Heaven meeting earth, in our homes, in our workplaces, in our own inner lives.

Looking to our desires—our strongest desires and our deepest desires—will help wake us up to our own souls. We must stop neglecting our hearts at the expense of hurry, weariness, and exhaustion. If we want to be fully alive and learn to live in the fullness of life that God offers, we must first look to what we are desiring and hoping for. We have to be willing to be honest with ourselves about what we're really longing for. It's okay if it hurts, if it opens an area of your heart that feels like it's too much to go there. God goes with you. He is with you in your longing, and it's your longing that will draw you close to Him.

Spiritual Practice

Write a list of all that you desire today. Now, comb through those desires and ask yourself what your deepest ones are. What's behind those strong desires?

Ask the Lord, "What do you want me to know about those deep desires?"

Then assess before the Lord if there are any areas in your life where you are wanting to be independent of Him and where you're wanting to decide what's good and bad in your own terms.

Ask God to align your desires with His, and pray this simple prayer: "Increase my capacity for You, God."

MADE FOR MORE

Has life left you weary and worn-out? Are you operating in survival mode? Have you neglected your heart because you've been so busy caring for everyone else's, or are you too scared to go there? Does it feel too daunting, too overwhelming to even open the door of your heart and longings because you're trying too hard to hold yourself together? Are you afraid that the moment you open that door, it will all unravel? Or have you opened that door, you were vulnerable, and you were let down?

You're being invited to open the door of your heart, to look at it with curiosity and tenderness, as the first step in becoming awake to your soul and healing.

But then what? What do we do when we look and only see exhaustion? How do we find peace?

How do we find freedom from trying to manage the outcomes?

How do we stay connected to our heart in the chaos of life?

How do we live from a place of deep desire and not just strong desire? How do we get honest with our desires and hold them out to the Lord in vulnerability and trust?

How do we truly delight in the life that we have, not the one we thought we would have, or are grabbing at, trying to attain?

Jeremiah 17:7–8 says, "Blessed is the man who trusts in the

LORD, whose trust is the LORD. He is like a tree planted by water, that sends out its roots by the stream, and does not fear when heat comes, for its leaves remain green, and is not anxious in the year of drought, for it does not cease to bear fruit."

This is a beautiful picture of our lives being compared to a strong, sturdy tree planted by living water.

But notice it says that the tree remains fruit bearing, sturdy, at peace *in the midst* of drought, *in the midst* of heat. Often, we want to be that sturdy tree in the middle of the most perfect California day where the sun is shining but it's not too hot, there's a slight breeze, and we're planted right by the stream of water that constantly flows and fills us. Then yes, of course we could flourish and produce fruit—if only we lived there in our souls. But Jeremiah doesn't say that. He says that the one who trusts in the Lord is firmly planted and fruit producing in the midst of the hard, dry, scorched places of life. See, the weather has changed and is not desirable. It's not what that tree would have signed up for or chosen. However, despite the hard, the tree is firmly planted and solid. And not only that, it is fruitful. This is a beautiful picture of hope for us. We cannot control the outcomes. We cannot manage how things will turn out. Hard and heat will come. However, we can be sturdy of soul when we trust in the Lord.

I think the reason why we so often neglect our hearts is because we don't see with the eyes of heaven. We are only seeing with earthly eyes. We only are seeing the right now, the temporal, the tangible. And so often we are mainly thinking of how we can survive.

Or we are striving to thrive.

But what if there's a better way? What if it doesn't involve striving at all? What if it's a light way, like Jesus promises in Matthew 11:28–30?

Society holds human flourishing as the highest value. I think most of us do as well. We long for peace, for a worry-free life, for happiness and truth and honesty. But the problem is that we are removing Jesus from it and holding it as the ultimate.

As believers, we don't operate in the same kingdom as society does. We live in the kingdom of God. Jesus tells us in John 10:10 that He came that He might give us life. What exactly does that life look like?

A little while ago, I was sitting with Jon Tyson, a pastor in Manhattan and a friend and mentor of ours, talking to him about this very thing. He looked at me and said this: "If I were to ask you what you really, really want, what would it be? Let me have a shot: You want good health, to go somewhere that gives you wonder, that wakes you up to a sense of possibility in the world; you want your kids to go to a school and be socially adjusted, to get to retirement and not be a burden to others. Right?"

I nodded.

"These aren't bad. But the pagan next to you who doesn't care about God wants the exact same things.

"You're not dreaming out of the imagination of heaven.

"*It's not that that's wrong; it's just that it's not enough for what you're made for.*"

As we pull back the curtain of our hearts and step out bravely by letting it be known, we must pull back the curtain of heaven and ask to see with the eyes of Jesus.

We are made for so much more.

God wants to give us so much more than what this world offers us, than what this world lures us with. Even the really good things of our hearts that we long for, they're not the ultimate. They're not the thing to give our whole lives over for, because the reality is, there's more. It's better. And it will never ever fail or disappoint.

But it's not something we can manage.

Rather, we must receive it.

In Philippians 3:7–8, Paul says, "Whatever gain I had, I counted as loss for the sake of Christ. Indeed, I count everything as loss because of the surpassing worth of knowing Christ Jesus my Lord. For his sake I have suffered the loss of all things and count them as rubbish, in order that I may gain Christ."

Pastor and author John Piper beautifully describes it in this way: "The key to magnifying Christ in life and in death is to find him more precious, more valuable, more satisfying, more joyful, more boast worthy than everything we lose in death—'to die is gain'—and everything we have in life—'to live is Christ.'"[1]

So what is the life that Jesus came to give us?

It's a life that is full of peace, joy, and love. It's a life full of delight. But a life that is only found in Jesus. He said, "I am the way, and the truth, and the life. No one comes to the Father except through me" (John 14:6).

He is the way.

Jesus.

We can't follow the five steps, we can't make it happen by our own will or attainment, we can't seek truth in our own self. It's as we look to Jesus, having the Spirit of truth in us as our Helper, that we will live the good life, where we find Jesus to be the most prized treasure, the one that we truly adore and long for. To live is Christ. To live is to be connected to Christ. We are in Him and He is in us.

The good life that you long for is not one you can manipulate. Rather, it's a relationship to step into and to receive. And in this relationship, not only will your heart become fully alive, but it will sustain you as you live life on earth with all of its beauties and all of its devastations.

C. S. Lewis says in *Mere Christianity*,

Your real, new self (which is Christ's and also yours, and yours just because it is His) will not come as long as you are looking for it. It will come when you are looking for Him. Does that sound strange? The same principle holds, you know, for more everyday matters. Even in social life you will never make a good impression on other people until you stop thinking about what sort of impression you are making. Even in literature and art, no man who bothers about originality will ever be original: whereas if you simply try to tell the truth (without caring two pence how often it has been told before) you will, nine times out of ten, become original without ever having noticed it. The principle runs through all life from top to bottom. Give up yourself, and you will find your real self. Lose your life and you will save it.[2]

And the context of this life that we find ourselves in is the world. We live in the kingdom of heaven, while occupying the spaces of earth. We live in the kingdom of heaven colliding with the kingdom of earth, and it's a here-but-not-yet kingdom. We live in the world, but we're not of it.

We must have the eyes of heaven to see. We must learn to behold the unseen and look past the seen.

There is a war going on. You are in a battle. Every day.

That's why you feel the tug to pursue the things of earth, trying to find your fulfillment and satisfaction here. That's why life feels hard most days. That's why you are disappointed and suffering and grieving. Because this is not our home and there is a battle going on.

Remember Genesis 1:1–2: God creates the world in a war, creating man and woman to partner together with Him to defeat darkness. To bring order where there is chaos, beauty where there is death, healing where there are wounds, hope where there is despair.

Jesus came to defeat Satan and death and sin, and we know who gets the victory in the end, but we are still in war. Satan is having his heyday.

We must open our eyes.

We must awaken to the war going on around us, so we can armor up and fight.

Fighting with the Holy Spirit's power, with the Holy Spirit's wisdom, with the Holy Spirit's help.

Jesus did not come for you to have self-care.

Jesus did not come so you can have every opportunity to be a girl boss.

Jesus did not come for you to live a well-adjusted and easy life that looks like you checked off all the marks on your journey.

Jesus came to win your heart back to His.

He came to free you from your sins and shame and fears and loss and hurt, and to make you whole and holy, so you can partner with Him in this war. He wants to partner with you in bringing goodness, love, justice, mercy, peace to this world.

Your desire to bring peace, joy, and love to others is good and what God calls us to, but it's as we partner with Him, as we are in Him, not as we do things on our own and try to hold it all together by how we manage it all.

He is looking for women who are fully devoted to Him. Who will lay down their lives, lay down their ideals, lay down their hurts and dreams and disappointments at His feet, to let Him care for them there. It's not that we minimize or push those aside, but rather we acknowledge them in the presence of God and go to Him with them. He is looking for women who lay down all the other loves that try to captivate their hearts and follow Him. He is jealous for you. He wants you. And He wants to hold your heart.

He wants you on His team.

We are so exhausted from managing outcomes because we love them more than we love Jesus. Our desires have become idols. We want to be married, we want our kids to be mature and do well in life, we want to be financially stable, we want to have friends and live at peace with others, we want to be liked and adored and loved and seen, we don't want to suffer, and we want it all more than Jesus.

Our desires become demands.

And our demands start to rule our hearts.

And so we neglect our hearts or try to earn our hearts, and we end up losing heart.

But Jesus came to give us fullness of heart.

In this world.

The problem is that this world is full of trials and tribulations. Jesus says in John 16:33, "I have said these things to you, that in me you may have peace. In the world you will have tribulation. But take heart; I have overcome the world."

And He prays in John 17:15–17, 22–23,

I do not ask that you take them out of the world, but that you keep them from the evil one. They are not of the world, just as I am not of the world. Sanctify them in the truth; your word is truth....The glory that you have given me I have given to them, that they may be one even as we are one, I in them and you in me, that they may become perfectly one, so that the world may know that you sent me and loved them even as you loved me.

We are meant to live on earth, with all of its trials and sorrows, with the Spirit within us. And by His power in us, we live on mission to do good using weapons of light.

Jesus didn't come to save us from the trials and pain; He came to be one with us and to *increase our capacity to go through trials* and come out with strength, hope, and joy.

The question is not how we can avoid suffering, how we can avoid pain, how we can have a good, easy, comfortable life.

The question is, how can we walk through the pain and the disappointments and the hard *with* Jesus, finding that He is our greatest love, peace, and joy? How can we stay firmly planted? We are saved from the pains of the natural consequences of sin as we walk with Him, but we also enter into the pain of others and share it in the name of Jesus. It is the cross of the believer, as well as the gift.

We can have love, peace, and joy because we have Jesus.

Jesus is love.

Jesus is peace.

Jesus is joy.

We can have defiant joy in the midst of the cruelest pain. We can have abundant peace in the midst of heartbreak and chaos. We can have delight and joy in the losses and sorrows of life because we are deeply loved by the King of the world, and no one and nothing can take that away from us.

Jesus came to give us fullness of heart by connecting us to His heart. Fullness of heart comes when we become one with Jesus, every day, choosing to draw near, choosing to be honest, choosing to surrender.

In one of Jon Tyson's sermons, "God Comes Where He's Wanted," Tyson poignantly describes how he wakes up every morning and cries out to God, "God, here I am. Look no further, your servant loves you and is looking to you. I am yours."

Second Chronicles 16:9 says, "For the eyes of the LORD roam throughout the earth to show himself strong for those who are wholeheartedly devoted to him" (CSB). This is holiness in action.

We can be transformed into women who have inner lives of love, peace, and joy while living outer lives that fight back the darkness. It's, in fact, only when we have inner lives of love, peace, and joy that we can go to battle.

We can't fight with our own strength.

With our own wisdom.

God wants to increase your capacity to be full of strength of heart, sturdiness of soul, and defiant joy in the midst of the war.

I had a call with my counselor this last week because, well, truth be told, I was stressed out of my mind. I wouldn't necessarily say I was consciously stressed, because I knew God was giving me all I needed for each day. But I was carrying around this burden of weight—I was so scared I would fall, that it would all fall apart, because I couldn't do it all.

I asked him, "I know that our bodies are meant to live under stress. So it's not always a question of how to get rid of the stress, but how do I do it in a healthy way? How do I get through this stressful season?"

I used to always think that I just wasn't supposed to be stressed, that stress was not of the Lord. (And then my professor reminded me of how Jesus had stressful moments. Let's all remember the Garden of Gethsemane and Jesus begging, pleading with the Father to take the cup from Him. Stress physically poured out of Him.)

But if you think about it, most days hold stressful moments. Some seasons much more than others. When we exercise, we are literally putting our bodies under stress, we are choosing stress, but we are doing so in order that our muscles may become strong, our hearts steadfast, and so our bodies can grow and increase in capacity.

There are things in our lives that we bring on ourselves that are stressful that we can let go of at the feet of Jesus. If we are doing too much, saying yes to too much, bearing the expectations of others, trying to manage everyone and everything, we can lay that down. (And do the harder work of being curious and searching for the why...more on that later.)

But there will also be times in our lives when we didn't choose the stress, but it's what we've been given, and we have to learn to live with it. Not in a survival way. But in a way where we are resilient. In a way where we have deep joy despite the overwhelm. Where we gain character and hope.

A lot of our lives will be like this.

The financial struggle that you didn't sign up for but can't seem to get out of quick enough.

The health diagnosis that is beyond your control.

The grief that came in the night and you couldn't stop.

The friendship that broke despite your best efforts.

The betrayal that you experienced, totally unexpectedly.

The heartache that you can't stop, no matter what you try.

The life stage you never imagined you'd find yourself in.

The chronic pain that you silently suffer.

The hope deferred that no matter what you pray, how much you try, or how long you wait is still not yet.

These are oh so real. So heartbreaking. So hard.

But we have a with-us God, Immanuel, who not only holds our sorrow for us but also goes with us in the sorrow. And although I don't believe He causes those pains, He will most assuredly redeem them. He will weave hope and healing into your story, no matter what your story holds. This is what God does. This is who He is. But it's only as you come to Him in those pains, in those disappointments, in those heavy burdens of life, crying out to Him, knowing that He can hold the pain with and for you.

In Exodus 33:12–15, Moses is talking to God and says,

> "Look, you have told me, 'Lead this people up,' but you have not let me know whom you will send with me. You said, 'I know you by name, and you have also found favor with me.' Now if I have indeed found favor with you, please teach me your ways, and I will know you, so that I may find favor with you. Now consider that this nation is your people."
>
> And he [God] replied, "My presence will go with you, and I will give you rest."
>
> "If your presence does not go," Moses responded to him, "don't make us go up from here. How will it be known that I and your people have found favor with you unless you go with us?" (CSB)

I can imagine leading a whole nation of stiff-necked, stubborn people was daunting for Moses. Maybe even not what he signed up for. He did it out of obedience to God, sustained by surrender to God. It was a hard task (understatement of the year).

But what I love here is how Moses is looking for *who*. How can he go alone? Who will help him? And he asks God to show him the way.

God could have responded by explaining that Aaron would help him—He eventually did give him another helper. He could have explained all the ins and outs of how it was going to go down. He could have given him a blueprint of answers. But instead, He gives Moses Himself.

I will go with you.

And I will give you rest.

We are at war, but we are not alone. God goes with us. And as we go, He will give us rest, although it's not the rest we think we need. It's not comfort or ease, but rather it's true soul rest.

In *The Lion, the Witch and the Wardrobe*, Mr. Beaver and Susan are having a discussion about Aslan, who represents Jesus:

"Aslan is a lion—*the* Lion, the great Lion."

"Ooh!" said Susan. "I'd thought he was a man. Is he—quite safe? I shall feel rather nervous about meeting a lion."...

"Safe?" said Mr. Beaver.... "Who said anything about safe? 'Course he isn't safe. But he's good. He's the King, I tell you."[3]

The life we sign up for in Christ is not a safe one. It's going to take a lot of risk. A lot of trust. A lot of honesty and humility. But we can fully embrace this life because the One we follow is *good*. There will be things that we grapple with and don't understand, may never understand, but God will prove Himself good to you. He is with us, always. He loves us, always, with such tenderness, care, and grace. He is with us in the midst of all the exhaustion, the heavy, the fragmented.

Do you want to know the answer my counselor gave me when I asked about stress and how to handle it?

He said, "First, you have to have a willingness to live with loss and failure. Stress is all about results. What-ifs, performance, how will it pan out? You have to learn to live with the results of tomorrow for whatever they are."

He then talked about staying connected to our souls. Our souls are meant to be sturdy and peaceful, while our bodies are meant to move and work and do. They do a lot! But our souls are the trunk of a tree, and they are intended to go slower. If we want to be anchored in our souls, we must slow down and tend to our hearts.

If our souls are the trunk of the tree, the branches above are the circumstances that sway in the wind. The branches can't control which way the wind blows, but as long as they stay connected to the trunk, they will make it through the storm.

Security comes with our sturdiness of soul.

Fullness of heart.

In the middle of the war. In the midst of pain and sorrow and disappointment. We must fight the idols of our hearts, see the unseen, and be devoted to Jesus, finding Him to be the greatest treasure of all.

In Exodus 34, after Moses goes back up the mountain to spend forty days and forty nights with God, he comes back down the mountain and Scripture says that "he did not realize that the skin of his face shone as a result of his speaking with the LORD" (CSB).

When we spend time with Jesus, seeking Him, we can radiate His light and His love to the world around us.

We can glow with His presence.

As we spend time with the Lord, learning, seeking, listening, and laying it all out before Him, what might seem like hard work and weariness will bring light and lightness. It will bring joy. It will bring a visible peace that may not even be as noticeable to you at first, like it wasn't to Moses, but those around you will see it. We reflect that which we revere. Do you revere God? Do you look to Him and choose to pour your heart out to Him, trusting that He will indeed meet you right where you're at?

Our spiritual transformation is not for our own peace and our own selves alone. Rather, it's to give God away. It's to fight back darkness in our homes, in our communities, in our cities. It's to see His glory, so we can reflect His glory to others. So others will join in on the war, fighting back darkness. Our light gives light. Freedom multiplies. Our fullness of heart causes ripples in the kingdom of heaven. It's not so we can sit and read our devotions with a warm cup of coffee overlooking the sunrise while the birds sing and there's worship music on in the background (although that is my ultimate favorite kind of morning). But it's so that as we sit in our true identities, as we receive and take hold of God's deep love for us, as we are healed and set free and lay down our idols, as we are comforted in our sorrow and pain, we can then go out and proclaim His glory and His goodness to others. We can be people of peace so they can know the One who is Peace. We can be women of joy so they can know the One who is Joy.

May we be women who let go of the outcomes we can't ultimately control, and may we reflect Jesus' light and love to those around us. Our presence brings His presence, and His presence is what changes everything.

Welcome to your divine glow-up!

Spiritual Practice

Go for a walk, or take out a journal, and ask yourself if there is anything you are demanding in your heart. Needs and desires are good and not wrong, but they become wrong when we demand them. Maybe it's one area, or one thing, or perhaps it's a list of things. How have you seen yourself trying to earn heart or losing heart because those demands have not come to fruition?

Take some time and confess, being honest with God about those demands. Surrender them to Him and ask Him to show you how He wants to give you fullness of heart through trust and surrender.

PART II

EARNING OUR HEARTS

Now we've seen how we can tend to neglect our hearts, pushing away the pain, pushing aside the longings, because it just feels like it's too much to go there. It's like opening Pandora's box: What will spill out?

But it is vital to our spiritual journey, to our health, to look at our desires and to consider our hearts and all that we are holding so we can start to truly live again. It's only as we begin to look at our hearts, to become self-aware, that we can begin the journey of healing and mending our souls. It's only as we "go there" that we can begin to have the imagination of heaven. It's only then that we will find rest and peace, knowing that we don't have to do it all, because He has already done it.

So now that we've begun the journey of self-awareness, let's look at how we try to earn our hearts. Let's see how we can look to control, approval, and ease in hopes of living lives of happiness and trying to manage all that has been given to us. However, each of these things only leaves us feeling more exhausted and worn-out. This section is all about laying down the go-to formulas in life in order to make room for God's better way of trust, delight, and mission.

5

THE ILLUSION OF CONTROL

The greatness of a person's power is the measure of their surrender. —WILLIAM BOOTH

How do you respond when you lose something? What do you do when life starts to feel out of your control, like you're on the losing team, and what you've been wanting, hoping for, working toward isn't working? When pain is knocking at the door, discomfort eases in, your plan is unraveling, and you are realizing that you cannot avoid losing that person, that job, that dream? That no matter your best efforts, no matter all the prayers, no matter that you're doing all the "right things," things still don't change? That you may lose what you have?

I think it's every person's tendency to want to try and control their circumstances. It's a humanity problem. It all started with the two people we first meet in the Bible—Adam and Eve—and Eve wanting to choose what was best for her life, what looked best to her, instead of trusting the Creator.

The *Oxford English Dictionary* defines *control* as "The fact or power of directing and regulating the actions of people or things."[1]

Cambridge Dictionary defines it as: "The ability or power to decide or strongly influence the particular way in which something will happen or someone will behave, or the condition of having such ability or power."[2]

We live in the age of influence. People are "influencers" as a job. We use the word as a noun, and we also say, "I was influenced," when we buy something online that an influencer talked about. I mean, let's be honest—I find most things these days because a friend mentions it, or someone I love online gives me the link.

"You have to have this lipstick. It's the best." Click. Buy.

"You need this collagen; it'll change your skin." Click. Buy.

"These shoes are the most comfortable. I wore them all over the city." Click. Buy.

Talking about products we love is not bad at all! I love learning little tips and tricks and things that work when a friend tells me about a product they're loving. But we have to be careful because often it's not even the product that we're really wanting, but rather what that product or person is promising. Same with clothing brands, or home goods, or anything that is sold to us. It almost has this underlying promise that *this* will satisfy us. *This* will change our lives. This will make our lives easier, our lives better, our lives more beautiful.

I mean, I look at my favorite clothing companies and think, *If I wear this, does it mean my life will look like this—glamorous, full of adventure, carefree?*

I look at my favorite home goods catalogs and think, *If I have this home, this furniture, will I be the greatest host? Will my home be brimming with peace and joy?*

If I buy this skin-care product, or this health product, will I have ageless skin that shines? Will I be able to always look in the mirror and be pleased by what I see?

We can so quickly buy into the lie that this thing is the answer to our problems, the solution, the key to happiness. And hear me— those things aren't always frivolous. I fully believe in taking care of our bodies, our homes, and our people. Sometimes I just need to know the most efficient way to clean my toilets or what broom works best for dog hair on my hardwood floors. Ya'll, we women gotta stick together and help each other out! But we have to always be looking to our motives. The reasoning behind what we do and if we're taking our eyes off Jesus. *Is this motive producing good fruit in me? Or bad fruit? Am I wanting to click on this because deep down I'm jealous and longing for their life? Am I relying on this thing or this way of living, or this formula to bring about the good life, or am I trusting God to meet me and fill me with Himself and have that be more than enough?*

Influence is not bad; it's actually really good because it's how we've been made. We were made for the influence of Christ to change us more and more into who He is. And in turn, to influence the world to know Him. This is kingdom work.

However, this goes south when we stop being conduits of Jesus' love and presence and start to think that it's our responsibility to manage the outcome, that it's our job to change people, to change circumstances, to step in and change the work of God because we think we know better. We can feel like it's all up to us to make the thing happen.

We start to control when we stop believing that God is sufficient.

Let me be clear: we do have responsibilities—to do the work, to pursue God, to seek transformation and change and wisdom. We are not victims of our circumstances. But we are meant to abide in Jesus, with Him as the vine and us as the branches, not the other way around.

So often we live as though we are gods of our own lives because we don't think He's loving enough, good enough, wise enough to lead us; we think we can do better.

We want Jesus to be our Savior, but not our King.

We want action. Now.

We want to be free of pain and discord and discomfort.

So we take matters into our own hands, trying to manipulate, control, and quicken the work in our lives that we hope for.

Last year was an extremely difficult one in our homeschool journey. It was shortly after moving into our new home, while we still had a long list of things that needed to be fixed and remodeled. It felt like not only was our outer life chaotic, but our inner home life was as well. One of our kids was deeply struggling, perfectionism and anxiety wreaking havoc at every assignment, causing so much discord and frustration. And I didn't know how to help. I tried everything. Grace upon grace. Letting things slide. Being calm and patient and understanding. Disciplining. Talking about consequences. Setting firm boundaries. (And in my most ungodly moments, yelling, throwing up my hands, exasperation reaching breaking levels.)

It wasn't just that homeschool was difficult; it was that my child was struggling, and I couldn't fix it. Nothing I did helped, it seemed. Instead of providing care and getting things done, our days often ended with both of us in our rooms crying and screaming, sometimes into our pillows, other times just out loud. I was so defeated, so discouraged, so full of shame.

This had gone on for months. It was getting harder, not better.

Why can't I figure this out?

Why do I keep losing it?

Why do they keep losing it?

Nothing is working.

I want out!

I showed up every day to face it, to do the work, to be present. I was obedient to the task at hand. I tried everything I could to change it—to change my child, to change me—to help the situation. But the reality was that it was completely out of my control, and that left me panicking.

Motherhood shows my temptation to control more than just about anything else. God commands Adam and Eve in Genesis 1:28 to "be fruitful and multiply and fill the earth and subdue it, and have dominion…" Humans are given the task to rule and subdue and to bring order to life. As mothers, we are tasked with bringing order and ruling our homes, but the problem is when we try to control the very things we have no authority over. When we try to control our kids' hearts and choices and actions. When we try to control their responses and words. Yes, they are under our shepherding and our care, but they have free will. We are tasked with setting the table, so to speak, with discipling and teaching and leading and caring, but at the end of the day, they choose what to do with all they've been given. They choose how to respond.

Perhaps you are in a different season, but I know control still knocks at your door. When it feels like you are behind in the day, behind in life. When your life is not what you thought it would be by now, it can be tempting to believe that if you do something in just the right way, follow some pattern, sign up for this program, your life can be easily fixed. It can be all that you hoped. *Your best life now!*

We can try and control what we eat, and how much we eat, and how much we exercise because we so long for that perfect body and feel like we haven't attained it. Or we tightly manage food because that's something we can control when other things feel out of control.

We can try and control what people think of us by what we share, how much we share, and by what we wear instead of coming just as we are, honest and free, with no pressure to appear in a certain way.

We can try and control the timeframes of our lives by having goals and saying yes or no to things depending on how they play into our five-year, ten-year, life plan. We leave no room for the Spirit to direct us; we leave no room for grace, for surprises and wonder. Or we wait around for our goal to come to fruition, wasting the time we've been given today.

But the reality is that control is just an illusion.

Jon Tyson says, "Despite our best efforts at playing God, things slip through our hands. Life cannot be tamed, God won't fit into a bottle, and our hearts are terrifyingly vulnerable to the world around us."[3]

We fear pain and loss, so we try to control.

We even try to control God.

We attempt to manage Him.

If I do this, then God will do that.

If you've grown up in the church, you probably grew up with great principles in life. But so many of us end up thinking of these not as principles but as rules to follow that will result in a good life. And when God doesn't act as we think He should, when He doesn't hold up His side of the bargain, when our best efforts don't produce the fruit we expected, we doubt God's character.

He must not love me.

He must not be good.

He must not be trustworthy.

Saint Ignatius of Loyola said that "sin is an unwillingness to trust that what God wants is our deepest happiness."[4]

But how do we reconcile that truth when it feels like life is anything but happy?

First, I think we need to redefine what we mean by happiness. We live in a nation whose primary value is happiness. Being happy in America is defined as whatever makes you feel good in the immediate moment, whatever eases your life, whatever brings a smile to your lips. But Jesus came and gave up His life for so much more than what eases you. He wants so much more for you than what feels good. He came to give you life—true, real, rich, abundant life. Happiness in God's economy is living with a full heart, a strong heart. It's knowing that despite the circumstances, despite the pain, you are full of such deep joy and gratitude and love and peace because you are full of God. This does indeed bring happiness, but a much deeper and richer happiness than what the world has to offer.

Remember our deepest desire is to connect to the heart of God and to become a person of love.

True happiness is not you getting your way, or controlling your circumstances so as to ensure you won't experience pain. Rather, true happiness is found in a relationship, and that can only be found in Jesus. My counselor says, "Purity of relationship is the goal. A lack of formula. To trust regardless of the circumstances."

When he told me this, I replied, "But I want the formula."

He laughed and said, "Of course. We long for a formula because we ultimately are longing for survival. But God wants so much more for us. He wants us to crave a relationship with Him, to crave grace."

Do we truly trust that He is who He says He is, even when life feels like He's not? Are we going to take God at His word? Are we going to remember what He has done, who He says He is, and what

He promises? This is the truth that we desperately need for our weary souls.

When I was talking about control with my counselor early this year, he recounted to me the story of Lazarus in John 11. Now, Lazarus was a friend of Jesus' and the brother of Mary and Martha. Mary is the same Mary who would sit at Jesus' feet, learning all that she could from her Rabbi (which was culturally wrong at the time in an honor-shame society—a woman learning from a rabbi—but Jesus broke through so many cultural barriers). She was the one who worshipped Him by pouring out expensive perfume on His feet and washing them with her hair. She adored Jesus; she loved Him above all else. The sisters had sent a messenger to tell Jesus that Lazarus was sick, and to come quickly and heal him. But Jesus didn't. He didn't answer them. He didn't come when they asked. And not because He didn't love him. John 11:3b says, "Lord, the one you love is sick" (CSB). Jesus deeply loved Lazarus.

I always got frustrated with Jesus when I read this passage. I'm always tapping my watch, telling Jesus, "Come on, Lord! Time is ticking away. Why aren't you doing something? Why aren't you rushing to his rescue? They need you."

And yet, He waited intentionally. The disciples knew that if He went to Judea, where Lazarus lived, He could be killed. The political climate was getting hot and Jesus was hated. However, Jesus didn't stay away because of fear. He held off because He wanted to glorify God.

Finally, after Lazarus had been in the tomb for four days, the exact amount of time that the Jews in that day believed the soul had parted with the body, Jesus came to Mary and Martha.

"Lord, if you had been here, my brother would not have died," cried Mary. Can't you feel her agony? The sorrow. The confusion.

I want to yell at my Bible, "Lord, you could have saved him! You could have prevented their grief!"

Jesus, seeing her weeping, and all those who were weeping around her, was deeply moved with compassion. The shortest verse in the Bible, it states, "Jesus wept" (v. 35). (My kids love quoting this verse!)

Can you feel the agony? The grief? The lament?

Jesus, if you had come when I asked, this wouldn't have happened. This pain would not be happening. People questioned Jesus. "If he could give a blind man sight, why couldn't he have kept this man from dying?" (see v. 37).

Jesus didn't prevent Lazarus from dying. But He did raise Lazarus from the dead.

John 11:43–44 says, "Jesus called in a loud voice, 'Lazarus, come out!' The dead man came out, his hands and feet wrapped with strips of linen, and a cloth around his face. Jesus said to them, 'Take off the grave clothes and let him go'" (NIV).

My counselor said at the end, "God is so other. It's very hard to figure out. What kind of love leads us into the desert of suffering, who doesn't intervene, heal, and resurrect right away, who allows for death and grief to be experienced? But we see here that nothing restrains love, even death doesn't separate us from love."

In this particular story, Jesus does finally intervene and raises Lazarus from the dead! I mean, it's incredible. But so often in our stories, that doesn't happen. Babies still die, cancer still strikes, divorce papers are signed, loneliness still prevails. Our days go all topsy-turvy, fights break out, exhaustion sets in.

I don't believe all of these things happen because God ordains them. We are living in a world where a very real enemy is at work, and many things are against God's will. It doesn't mean God is not powerful or can't intervene; it just means that although we know who has the victory in the end, there is still a very present battle going on.

But the question still remains.

Who are you trusting in?

Yourself?

Or God?

And if you trust in God, is He trustworthy?

We sing, "Lord, I surrender all," but do we really? Can we? Isn't that the scariest place to be?

Giving up everything, laying it down, feels so counterintuitive to our try-harder, can-do, fix-it, manage-it selves.

And yet, that's who God is. He is the God of exchange. He takes our surrender and gives us release. He takes our worry and gives us peace. He takes our fears and gives us faith that sturdies our souls.

He asks us to surrender, knowing it's not easy but promising to give us a light burden in exchange.

Who are we surrendering to? Only the most trustworthy, good, wise, and gracious King that ever was and is. Oh, it's scary because it's a letting go with no promises of a good outcome, but it is a letting go that gives tenfold back. Not necessarily a tenfold back of material good or even what you are praying for, but it gives intimate relationship, strength, hope, grace, and peace.

Learning to surrender our lives, our days, our relationships, our kids, our futures, our finances, our health, our desires and longings and hurts and pains to the One who raises the dead and who died on our behalf is the journey we are called to. We are called to trust the One who surrendered it all even though he could have not gone to the cross, but rather he bore the greatest of our pains and griefs so that we could have true life.

He does not ask us to do anything He has not done first.

Jesus surrendered it all to God on the cross.

And His surrender resulted in a great glorification, for all of us.

To surrender is to have a posture of openhandedness. It's an "on your knees, with tears running down your cheeks, laying it all out before God" kind of posture. It's opening up your tight fists and releasing the burdens and the cares into His capable and good hands. It's to bind yourself with God and receive His easy and light yoke because you know it's not up to you to have the right outcome. It's a life lived in trust and faith that often feels like a free fall. As Robert Mulholland, a professor of theology, states, it's a "free me from the care of myself" type of walk, where we can truly release the care of our lives to the One who cares for us.[5]

We are not only surrendering to a God who is trustworthy, but we are surrendering to the only One who can hold all of our pain and sorrow because He became sorrow for us.

God is not just after our obedience; He is after our surrender. He can take your questions, your doubts, your cries, your concerns— but He wants you to keep coming back to Him with them, and as you do, your heart will slowly trust more and more. You can obey with a heart that is shut off, but you can't surrender without a heart that is fully trusting. Without knowing the goodness and grace of the One whom you are surrendering to. This is not a passive surrender. He is after your yes. Your willingness to trust Him no matter the outcome. To obey what He says because you are in relationship with Him and love Him.

Do you love Him more than the outcome?

To be honest, our homeschool year didn't end well. In fact, I ended it early because neither one of us could go on any longer. I tried applying for the local private school here for the next year, but it was too late (apparently applications start in the fall of the prior year!). But that summer the Lord did what only He could as we took a break and learned how to just enjoy each other again. We adventured, had late summer nights reading and watching movies, and spent our days in the sunshine. I would go for my daily walks, crying out to God for wisdom and provision. The thought of homeschooling again left my nerves in fitful balls. But as the summer progressed, as I drew near to Him, He comforted my heart with His truth—that motherhood was a gift, and although I fell short every day, I was not alone. I was equipped with the power of His Holy Spirit, and He loved me and loved my child more than I could ever imagine. As I tended to my own heart, as I played and rested and met with my counselor and prayed with friends who loved my child, I began to open my hands and heart in surrender.

To accept what was, instead of fighting for what I thought should be.

It broke every ideal I had about homeschooling. It did not look like time spent under shady trees for long hours reading rich literature and eating homemade cookies while I wore a cute dress and sat on a handsewn quilt and my kids looked at me with delight like the Von Trapp kids looked at Maria up in the hills of Austria as she sang "Do-Re-Mi." (Y'all, this is truly what I thought homeschooling would be like!) No, ours was a real life, cuddled around the kitchen island in our pajamas until noon, syrup on the counters, learning but having it hard-won. I had to learn to surrender my child to the Lord and allow Him to do what only He could do. I can be present; I can love fiercely and pray fervently and constantly share about the goodness of God, and ask for forgiveness when I sin, and show them the grace of God, and delight in them by smiling and looking into their eyes. But I cannot change their hearts. I cannot make them obey or fix their anxiety.

But my God can.

And He did.

We asked a few of our mentors to pray for our child for thirty days and to let us know if they heard anything from God. And y'all, this child was completely different by the end of the month. Softhearted, receptive, free, delight on their face, able to look us in the eyes.

Now, we may have seasons like this again, and it may take much longer than thirty days, but we got to witness the kindness and mercy of God. I will forever be in awe of God's kindness that leads us to repentance, of His mercy that is new every morning, of His power that can move a mountain, and His love that makes a heart of stone turn to a heart of flesh.

Of course, my kids are little still, and I am smack-dab in the middle of motherhood, learning and longing and praying my way through these days. (I wonder if that ever changes as a mom.) My kids' stories are still being written; my story is still being written. I know we will face challenges in the future that are out of my control. My kids are not robots for me to manipulate, but they are humans with wills (and longings, desires, and ideas; I pray that above all, they learn to trust in Jesus with their whole hearts and live faithfully with and for Him with great boldness).

There are still other things in my life that are out of my control. Still other longings that I am waiting on. Breakthroughs, heart cries. Things in my marriage, things in my body, things in my family, things in my community. I am walking with friends who are going through deep suffering—in their homes, in their marriages, in their health. So many things feel completely out of control. They seem irreparable, not fixable, daunting.

My temptation is to fix it! Solve it. Save it.

But then I hear this still, small whisper: *Do you trust Me?*

I have to not sweep it under the rug but let Him deal with it. It's a hard-earned trust. (Sounds like an oxymoron, but it's not.) A trust that comes by searching my own heart, and the areas that feel pained and unsettled, and asking God, "Lord, what do you want me to know? Is there anything you want me to do?"

Our job is not to change the person, to fix the situation, or to make everyone happy. We don't have to make "it" happen, whatever "it" is in your current situation.

Rather, it's to open up our heart to the King of the universe and let Him do what only HE can do. To let Him do all that is in His heart to do—in us, in our people, in our circumstances.

And as we open up our hearts to Him, asking, being honest, pleading, and choosing to trust His work, we become women who can live freely, with grace. It doesn't always look graceful as we do it. Sometimes it looks like mascara-stained cheeks and puffy eyes and big-lettered journal entries and running with Jonas Brothers blasting in your earphones while you punch the air!

But as you cry out, as you lay it down, as you open your hands and your heart, He will replace your heavy burden with His light yoke, as Matthew 11 promises.

The word *yoke* here is an agricultural term. Think of *Little House on the Prairie*. A farmer puts two oxen together using a piece of wood; this is the yoke. The yoke would join the two animals so they could work together. This term throughout the Bible depicted slavery, having a heavy load and a hard burden. But in Matthew 11, Jesus talks about how the Lord longs to join us on the journey, and to bear the weight together. But here's the thing. He doesn't only bear it with us; He also shoulders it for us. Life with Jesus is a burden-light life. Not that it will be easy, but that we don't have to bear the weight of the outcome any longer. We can be joined together with God as He shoulders our heaviness and in exchange gives us a light bag. The word *easy* in Matthew 28:30 means that it will be good and kind. It's not saying our lives will be lived with ease, but rather, as we walk with God through the hard, He will make it good and kind. This is His promise for you, for me. This is His invitation. Not that the burden goes away, but that God gives us His yoke, uniting us to work the hard land, shouldering the burden for us, and giving us a light load. We journey and work together with the Father, not alone.

Look at the following graph and consider what we cannot control and what we can have influence over. Are there any areas you are trying to control that are not up to you?

CHECKLIST: WHAT YOU CAN HAVE INFLUENCE OVER AND WHAT YOU CANNOT CONTROL

I recently bought some "feeling" posters for my kids from Amazon recommended by *Are My Kids on Track?*[6] Honestly, I'm still learning how to discern what I'm feeling and how to express it, and I need all the help I can get to teach my kids to name their feelings and emotionally regulate. When I was hanging up the posters on our big chalk wall, one of them caught my eye. It was about control, and I thought, *Wow, I need this reminder just as much as (maybe more than!) my kids.* Of course, the poster I bought is really cute with colors and graphics, but I find myself referencing it often enough that I wanted to share it with you, for when you feel the temptation to control outcomes and people and circumstances. Here is my rendition of what we have influence over, and what we cannot control.

Things I Have Influence Over
- My thoughts: "Take every thought captive" (2 Cor. 10:5). God gives us the power to dwell on what is good and true. We cannot always control what thoughts pop into our head, but we can choose which thoughts we let stay and get cozy in our minds and which ones we open the door and kick out. We must be vigilant to kick out the unwanted

thoughts that will leave us anxious, fearful, insecure, and bound.

- My boundaries: Boundaries may feel uncomfortable, but they are good. They protect us from exhaustion, from harm, from being diminished. Some seasons, some relationships will need more boundaries than others. Take inventory of areas of your life that need more boundaries so you can live more freely.

- My words: "For the mouth speaks out of that which fills the heart" (Matt. 12:34 NASB). It is our job to be careful and wise with what we choose to nourish and fill ourselves with, because whatever we put into our minds and bodies and hearts will come out through our words. We have the choice to speak blessing or cursing. There is no neutrality. You can choose to speak life or death.

- My behavior: I'm always telling my kids, "Regardless of what someone else does, you are responsible for your actions." We get to choose how we will respond to people and situations. The more we walk with Jesus, the more we spend time with Him and are cared for by Him in His gentleness, the more we will be able to respond to life with a gentle spirit.

- Asking for help: We are never helpless! Ask for help. Ask the Lord, ask a friend, ask a mentor, ask a pastor—ask.

- My choices: We are responsible for the choices we make; no one else can make them for us.

- My friends: We get to choose whom we surround ourselves with. Are we getting sharpened and encouraged by the people we spend time with? Or do they bring us down?

- Expressing my feelings: We don't need to express our feelings perfectly. There's no right or wrong way, but we get to be honest with ourselves, with the Lord, and with those that are safe for us to talk with about how we are actually doing.

- My goals (surrendered to God, at His pace): We get to choose what to dream of, go after, and lean into. If you are walking with Jesus, then your deep desires are good and godly and there's freedom of what to choose to pursue. We get to choose our goals, but we must place them in the Father's hands.

Things I Cannot Control

- The future: No matter how hard we try, we can't control what will happen. There's no safeguarding against what the future entails. We must learn to be okay with whatever tomorrow will bring.
- Other people's ideas: People will think things that are different, and sometimes no matter how charismatic, how smart, how well-laid-out your ideas are, they won't change theirs. We have to let them have their own ideas.
- The past: What happened in the past—perhaps the hurt or sin that was done to you, or by you—is in the past. We can't go back and change it, but we can change how we experienced it. Sometimes that's going back into those moments with a counselor or with the Holy Spirit and inviting Jesus onto the scene to show us where He was, what He wants us to know, to imagine redemption.
- Other people's feelings: No matter how hard we try, we cannot control how people will respond to us or how they will feel. It is not your responsibility to make them happy. You can be committed to their happiness, but you are not responsible for it.
- The weather: No matter how much we track the weather, it is totally out of our control. We must receive what it brings, no matter our plans.
- Other people's thoughts: We cannot control what people will think. Sometimes that may mean that we need to accept being misunderstood and stop trying to change how they perceive us.
- Other people's mistakes: People will make poor choices, and that is not our fault. How can we love them and show

grace and mercy in the midst of those moments, while also being truthful to the consequences of those mistakes?

- Other people's actions: People have a will and will choose to act in ways that we cannot control. The question is how will we respond to them?
- Other people's opinions: People will think what they think, and sometimes you may totally disagree with them, or their opinion may greatly affect you. They are allowed to think what they think, but how will we show grace and love and care in the midst of perhaps the disunity? However we love, we are not responsible for their opinions.

Spiritual Practice

When you look at your life, is there something that you've been holding back from God? One thing you've been trying to control and figure out on your own? Maybe you're not ready yet to talk to God about that particular thing, afraid it will be too painful.

I encourage you to go there. Don't hold back. Write it down in a journal, say it to one person.

And commit to praying for that thing for thirty days. Ask three people whom you trust and who love God to pray about that with and for you and ask them to write down anything they hear from the Lord on that topic, any verses that come to mind, any visions they have.

Then give thanks for what God does in those thirty days.

6

SEEKING TO PLEASE

I had never experienced rejection like that.

Sure, there were times when I hadn't made the team, hadn't gotten the part in the school play, or wasn't chosen by the boy I had crushed on for years. But to lose someone so close, someone whom I loved and adored, who loved Jesus, felt like more than I could bear.

Times three.

Three relationships in one year. Three relationships that were close and full of love and kindness completely fell out from under me.

One after another.

All for different reasons. All in different ways. Each took different lengths of time. But all three ended without closure and all of them created such a great chasm of loss in my life. I wasn't guiltless in them, but it also seemed like no matter what I did, I couldn't conjure up the ending I was hoping for.

I remember the day that I got the voice message. I was at my favorite local coffee shop, grabbing my oat milk vanilla latte, when I saw a voice note pop up on my phone. It was from one of my favorite people, so I quickly clicked on it, excited to hear from her. Instead of hearing a sweet update, or a heartfelt prayer request, or a "Hey, just thinking of you today," I listened to her accusing me of false motives. I remember the pain so apparent in her voice, pain that I was unaware that I had caused. My heart sank. My throat went dry. I went into total denial, getting in the car, driving home, thinking, *Surely this can't be happening. Surely this isn't real. I'll have to call her and sort it all out. I'm sure she'll understand; we just need to talk to one another.*

I left a voice note that night, sharing my heart, apologizing, begging to hop on the phone with her to talk. But I heard nothing.

The next day, my mind started to spiral, my nerves started to shake, and I was not okay.

I spent the afternoon in our guest room, wailing to the Lord. It felt like my heart had been ripped open.

How could she think that of me?

How could she say that about me?

Where did I go wrong?

How could I make it right?

How did I miss it?

I went to the depths of despair, spiraling.

How do you handle getting shot at with accusations? How do you repair a friendship that utterly breaks in a matter of twenty-four hours?

As I thought and prayed, I saw holes where I had been insensitive and needed to ask for forgiveness. I saw how I could have possibly prevented the situation by communicating and pursuing more. The accusations weren't all false. They held some weight of truth to them.

I was able to talk with her a few days later, and the conversation was kind and genuine, but even so, the friendship was irreparable. It had broken beyond mending.

Oh, how I wished I had done things differently. How I lamented the way things went. I grieved for months.

Depression seemed like a dark cloud filling my mind day and night.

It was a breakup of the most devastating kind.

And to be honest, all three breakups were devastatingly awful.

How could this have happened?

Where did I go wrong?

I constantly played back in my mind all that I had done wrong in each friendship. The things I wished I could have done differently. The things I wished I would have said. The things that I wish they'd responded with. Over and over my mind looped. I woke up thinking about it, and I went about my day—dishes, getting ready, homeschooling my kids, working out, cooking dinner—thinking about it. And most nights, I went to bed replaying it all in my mind.

It was a constant loop, never ending, and slowly, day by day, it began to shackle me.

Shame became a close friend.

I started to believe the lie *You are a terrible friend.* I mean, I believed it to my core. *I am a bad friend.*

You're too needy.

You're not enough.

You're selfish.

I began to sink away from community because I was so terrified of being rejected again, of others feeling like I betrayed them.

I want to have tough skin and a soft heart. But how do you do that when your heart feels like it's been wrung out to dry? I felt like a burn victim, with my skin too sensitive to even be touched.

I started to pray every day from Psalm 139:23–24: "Search me, O God, and know my heart! Try me and know my thoughts. And see if there be any grievous way in me, and lead me in the way everlasting!"

I became so fearful of sinning that I would beg God to show me if there was any hidden sin in my heart that I wasn't seeing. Beg Him to show me how to make it right, how to prevent it from happening again. But as I continued to pray this, I became more fearful. What if I'm missing something? What if there's something in me that I don't see? What if people aren't telling me something that is blatantly true?

My worst-case scenario had become a reality. I have always worried about people not liking me. I have always struggled with my people-pleasing tendencies. The Lord has been so gracious with me over the years, breaking that down in me and changing me to long to follow Him above all else. But the truth was, I had believed the formula that if I was nice, sweet Alyssa, no one would ever be mad with me, no one would ever not like me or have a reason to hate me.

Nice/nonconfrontational/sweet = accepted, liked.

And yet, that formula unraveled before my very eyes, and it hit my heart hard.

The Lord surrounded me with a few friends during this time—people who are still my dearest friends today—who spoke life and truth over me.

I remember telling my friend Emilie about being so afraid of sinning against others or needing to make further amends for these relationships with no closure. She said very clearly, "Alyssa, if you are asking the Lord to show you your heart, and if there is any sin, He will. He would never withhold that from you. He loves it when we ask Him for purity of heart, so you can trust that if He hasn't shown you anything, then there is nothing to be seen."

It was like a wave of relief washed over me. God was not with-holding anything from me. I was in the light.

It was this same friend, along with my other friend Emily (with a *y*) and my mentor Tammy, who still to this day continually tells me, "Alyssa, you are a good friend." I still get tears in my eyes when I hear it, because that lie had been so embedded into my heart.

I had thought that I could earn strength of heart by earning love from others. I thought if I was nice and sweet and never stepped on anyone's toes, I would be liked and loved. I thought I could earn love by pleasing people, which in turn would make me whole. I wanted to please others to prevent pain, and to find my security in people liking me.

However, when I couldn't hold it together, when the friendships unraveled before my eyes no matter what I said or tried to do, I felt like my world had fallen apart. And in the falling, the enemy whispered lies that sunk into the very fibers of my being.

Satan wants to destroy us. He wants to whisper lies into our ears that we will grasp on to and make agreements with. And oftentimes, it's all in our minds, so that lie becomes isolated and alone with no light or truth to reveal it. He wants to keep us alone in our questions, guilt, and shame. And those lies become identities that we hold on to, that are straight from the pit of hell.

We cannot choose what is spoken to us or over us. But we do have agency to choose what we do with what is thrown at us, given to us, or whispered to us. Good or bad. Agency is the power we have to choose what we will do with what we're given.

A lie, an accusation—choose to believe it or reject it in the name of Jesus.

A truth, an encouragement—choose to agree with it and make it our own or reject it in the name of insecurity or pride.

Because here's the thing: even the truth that is spoken over us that is good and right and uplifting we cannot receive as our own if we do not make it our own.

My counselor described it to me once like a pocket. You can collect as many rocks as you want—all encouragements and good words from the Lord, Scripture, mentors, your friends—but if you have a hole in your pocket, you'll lose them all. You won't take them as your own. Is your pocket holding truth?

We have the choice to agree with truth or lies. We have the choice to agree with the enemy or with God. We can't control which lies get spoken over us, but we can choose to reject or receive them.

And yes, we need people to remind us of truth and lead us and help us in wisdom, but we have to accept it for ourselves.

Both rejection and praise can lead us away from God if we do not collect them with His pocket. Even the praise of people, as much as we're called to encourage others, can become a trap. We can start to base our value, our worth, our goodness on what others say or believe about us.

Bob Sorge in *Dealing with the Rejection and Praise of Man* says, "You won't be healed of rejection by analyzing the source of your rejection but by looking at the source of your acceptance."[1]

We must know what God says about us and let that be our firm foundation. But here's the thing: We have to receive His truth. Not just know it. We have to receive it for ourselves.

Do you really believe you are God's beloved?

Do you really believe that you are loved unconditionally?

Do you really believe that God delights in you, regardless of your performance? Of what you do?

Do you really believe that you are a treasure because you are

His image bearer and child, not because of what you can bring to the table?

Whose voice holds the most weight in your life? Are you living for the praise of others, or the praise of God, who already delights in you? Is there a voice that is weighing you down?

With these broken friendships, I had to learn to move on even when there was no closure. I had to learn to quiet the voices of those who seemed to not like me, or rejected me, or weren't pleased with me, and turn up the volume of God's voice—the voice that really mattered. I had to learn to receive God's love and have that be more than enough for me—a love that is not earned but that is free and full.

This was not easy for me! I am by nature a peacemaker and hate conflict. And here I was, face-to-face with conflict. I had to learn to have difficult conversations with people who felt hurt by me, and whom I felt hurt by as well, and rest in knowing I did the right thing in the Lord's eyes, even if it didn't produce the outcome I would have hoped for. I had to confess areas of sin that I needed forgiveness for, and the hardest part was being honest about my feelings—the areas that deeply hurt me. I had to learn to live with people who were still displeased by me.

I had operated for so many years keeping quiet, thinking I was being nice, but really, I hurt myself and others by not being up-front, honest, and open. By living in the gray, by not being honest when I was hurt and letting that hurt grow into bitterness or resentment. And for so long, I wasn't truly honest with myself. I tried to just be "okay" so I would stay steady, but the reality is "okay" is not steady. Rather, digging out the truth and bringing it to light is what makes us truly steady. Stuffing it just makes us a ticking time bomb.

I had to learn to entrust myself to Jesus, the only One who gives unconditional love, a love that I can rest secure in, and let that love fill me so I can love others—learning to be vulnerable once again, to take risks once again, but this time, not in fear of what someone will do or say or not do or say, but out of love and security in Jesus.

One of my greatest fears in life was being rejected by others, them not liking me. And it happened. My greatest fear became my reality. I failed.

I hurt.

And at the end of the day, I was okay.

In fact, I was good, eventually.

Because with so much loss, I had to turn to Jesus. He was all I had. He was the One I ran to to hold my heart, to speak truth over me, to walk with me through the pain.

I had been concerned with managing my friendships in such a way that there wouldn't be conflict, so that my friends wouldn't be displeased with me or—the worst thought imaginable—hurt by me. But regardless of my best efforts, I hurt them, and the friendships fell apart. And in the falling, the Lord gave me the greatest gift of all—deep friendship with Him.

Jon Tyson gave this advice around the fire one night at our house: "Learn to befriend loneliness." Whether it's because we don't fit in, have been pushed out or dropped, or because we haven't met anyone to walk life with us yet, we must learn to befriend loneliness. Which sounds like an oxymoron, doesn't it? Who would want to do that? Loneliness can be painful, scary, quiet. But here's the truth: you are never alone. You may feel lonely, but God is always whispering, "I will never leave or forsake you. I am with you, to the ends of the earth" (see Heb. 13:5 and Matt. 28:20).

Deuteronomy 31:6 says: "Be strong and courageous. Do not be

afraid or terrified because of them, for the Lord your God goes with you; he will never leave you or forsake you."

Loneliness stops being scary when you welcome Jesus into it. When you get away with Him and discover who He is, who you are, and who you are together. And it's only in that place that you can realize that Jesus is, in fact, more than sufficient. And it's not until you accept that that you can truly then love people fully, without insecurity, without strings, without unhealthy needs, and become fully present to them, fully able to give yourself to them with a full heart.

Others had rejected me, but Jesus welcomed me. Friendships had fallen apart, but Jesus held me together and drew closer to me through the falling out.

He became the One I talked with in the morning when I woke up, journaling and listening to His voice. He was the One I talked to in the afternoon as I went for my walk, feeling His nearness and His presence. He was the One I would cry to in the night, who would comfort me and remind me of His goodness.

So often, I heard Him tell me, "Alyssa, I love you. How's your heart? You are so precious to me. You are my treasure. I am so proud of you. I delight in you. I love being with you."

Trevor Hudson quotes M. Basil Pennington, a Catholic priest and monk, in his book *Beyond Loneliness*, saying, "Prayer is friendship in action—that high point of friendship when we are simply entering into and experiencing the reality that we and God are friends."[2]

I think we often feel like prayer is a chore, or we don't do it because we don't know how. But prayer is the way we become friends with God, just like human friendships are deepened by sharing our stories and feelings and questions. God wants to be your friend. He longs to have a deep friendship with you.

Trevor Hudson says, "Whatever makes for good friendship makes for good prayer."[3]

I learned to walk with God. Day in and day out. In the mundane, in the quiet, in the busy.

Dallas Willard shares about his journey of becoming more and more full of Jesus in his biography, and he talks about how he started to say these three simple words throughout the day:

"I receive You."[4]

As he took a breath in the middle of his lectures at USC, he'd pray, "I receive You." As he finished grading a paper and before starting another, he'd tell the Lord, "I receive You."

The Christian life is one of receiving. God wants to give you His whole self. He wants you to be full of Him. To fully receive Him. He does not withhold His presence from those who are seeking Him.

God was with me always, and because I knew I was *secure* in Him, I could be vulnerable with all my hurt and questions and pain, and rest in His unconditional love for me.

The thing that was so shocking about those broken friendships was that I had always thought that if I was "perfect" (nice enough, sweet enough, never messed up), no one would ever be displeased with me. I wouldn't hurt people. I would never lose anyone.

If I could just get it right, then I'd be okay.

But I learned that even when we do them right, things can still fall apart.

I learned that I indeed cannot get it perfect all the time, and that even if I could, that wouldn't ensure others' approval.

Jesus was perfect, and yet so many people hated Him.

Jesus was perfect, and yet so many betrayed Him.

Jesus was perfect, and yet so many rejected Him.

Jesus was, in fact, born into rejection. We're all familiar with Jesus' birth story that is told every Christmas: how when Mary and Joseph traveled to Bethlehem for the government census, there "was no place for them in the inn." Joseph was going back to where his family was from, from the line of David, and you can be assured that he had family in town. In the ancient Jewish culture, family was everything. It was not like the individualized and independent America. If your family came to town, you most definitely would welcome them into your home and make a place for them. However, because Mary was very much pregnant and not married to Joseph, this brought great shame to their family in this shame-honor culture, and so they were not welcomed into the town. Therefore, she gave birth in the animal barn, almost like giving birth in your family's garage (and not the nice, remodeled kind that has shelves and that block carpet for workouts). Cold, inhumane, outside.

Jesus served and loved and always did the right thing, and yet He still was led to the cross, was mocked and ridiculed, rejected. A man of sorrows.

We must learn to find our security in Jesus, regardless of the praise or the rejection that comes from others. Emilie gave me this vision of me a year before all of this happened: She described me standing on a rock in the midst of the ocean. There was a long, shallow tide, like the ones on the Oregon Coast that go out for miles. She said that as I stood there, I was standing on the rock of Jesus, so whether the current came in with the praise of others, or went out with the disapproval of others, my firm footing did not move. I was standing on the firm foundation of Jesus.

I think the idol of approval is rooted in fear and pride: *What will they think of me? Will they misunderstand me? Will they reject me? Will they like me?* But really, when it comes down to it, it's the fear of loss and suffering: *Will I lose them? Will I suffer the loss of my reputation, my identity, my social circles, my friendship?*

You might. I did. But let me tell you, choosing to do the right thing, choosing to have the hard conversation, choosing to put up the boundary if needed, to apologize, to do whatever you can to be at peace, even if it doesn't end as you had hoped, is worth it. You are not alone as you seek to do all that you can do to be at peace with others. You can only be responsible for your part in it.

Daniel is one of my favorite Bible characters. A man who was different, set apart. He was willing to look weird to please the Lord. He went against the culture and kept his face toward the Lord. He got thrown into a den of lions, and yet God spared his life, and he became friends with the lions. It could have been so tempting to go along with the culture in order to stay in favor with the king. It could have been so easy to act how he was expected to and still follow Jesus in the quietness of his heart, except he knew that wouldn't be holy. That wouldn't be fully devoted to God. He stood up, spoke up, and fought against the approval of man. And you know what is so ironic? He did gain the favor of man. But only because God gave it to him.

Daniel 1:8–9 says, "But Daniel resolved that he would not defile himself with the king's food, or with the wine that he drank. Therefore he asked the chief of the eunuchs to allow him not to defile himself. And God gave Daniel favor and compassion in the sight of the chief of the eunuchs."

Daniel asked him if he could just eat vegetables and drink water, instead of the king's food. But this was absurd. He was in training for the next three years to be in the king's court, to be educated, strong, and mighty. It would look bad for the king if Daniel started to lose weight and wither away on this measly diet. The chief of the eunuchs granted Daniel's request hesitantly, and instead of looking weak, Daniel looked better than all the others who were feasting on the best of food! Shadrach, Meshach, and Abednego (the three who entered the blazing fire unscathed in Daniel 3) also took part in Daniel's fast.

Daniel 1:15 says, "At the end of ten days it was seen that they were better in appearance and fatter in flesh than all the youths who ate the king's food."

Now before you start in on a Daniel fast to gleam like Daniel did, this is not a plea for this particular diet, but rather it was a complete miracle! Daniel did the opposite of what you would do to build strength and look youthful by fasting and saying no to good things so that he would rely more heavily on God and hear from Him. Daniel's appearance was fully nourished, robust, healthy. When we follow God, when we spend time with Him and let His voice be the one that speaks over us, it transforms us from the inside out. To the world, it doesn't make sense, but in God's kingdom, we actually become stronger, more confident, shining with His glory. Daniel walked with God, and not only was he a friend of God, but he was also able to participate in amazing acts for God!

Psalm 25:14 says, "The friendship of the LORD is for those who fear him." *The Message* says it this way: "God-friendship is for God-worshipers; they are the ones he confides in."

God confides in the ones who seek Him. He talks to us, befriends us, draws us near. His friendship is the one that gives beauty and grace to all other friendships. And His is one that will never come to an end, no matter how messy it gets or life gets. Pursuing friendship with the Lord is one of the most glorious privileges of a believer.

Bob Sorge says this in *Dealing with the Rejection and Praise of Man*:

So prepare yourself. You'll never grow beyond the need for rejection to tenderize your heart before God. When you view rejection as a gift from God to keep your heart pliable and dependent upon him, you gain a new freedom in relating to people in love. Even though you know people are not dependable, you are able to give yourself to them in unqualified love, knowing that any rejection you receive from them is an opportunity for character development. When people reject you, but you are fueled on the inside with the profound affections of your Father for you, then you're able to give yourself to your fellow man in love regardless of how he treats you.[5]

Oftentimes we are left completely exhausted because we are relying so heavily on others' approval of us. We are looking to people, even our best of people, to fill us and give us acceptance and value. This is idolatry. The only sure foundation is friendship with Jesus. Yes, we are called to love others wholeheartedly, to serve them and care for them. But our wholeness of heart can only come from our acceptance in Jesus. Then, and only then, can we become people who are free and can let love freely flow through us, because our love is not based on their approval, but on God's acceptance of us.

Spiritual Practice

Spend some minutes talking to God as a friend. Tell Him how you are feeling—angry, disappointed, hurt, scared. He not only knows your pain, but He wants to hold it with you. Tell Him the details of your heart as much as you can. And tell Him as a friend, not expecting Him to fix it but to be present with you. This is not an intercessor prayer, but a friendship prayer where you enter into the safety of His presence.

God accepts you just as you are today. He delights in you. Are there any truths from His Word, or truths that others have spoken over you, that you haven't accepted? How can you mend your pocket and truly receive those truths as your own? After you have that one truth—or a few—say it out loud. Confession with our mouth is a way we can practice agency.

7

EVERYDAY EASE

Jeff got us a cold-plunge tub this summer. For years we were against the fad. My idea of hell is being cold, so I clearly had no desire for it whatsoever.

We've been on a health journey after a really scary year with Jeff's health, and frankly, our bodies just aren't what they used to be. Jeff had been told that this might help, so we... well, we took the plunge! (Ba-dum tsh!)

Jeff had been waiting months for this big ol' tub to show up on our front doorstep, and finally the day came.

I was not excited about it. I thought it'd be great for him, but there was no way I'd join him.

Until Emilie, who can sell me anything by her charisma, raved on and on about the cold plunge.

"It'll change your life!" she promised.

"Just stay in for forty-five seconds, and just you wait and see. But don't get out before that. You'll feel amazing, Alyssa!"

After Jeff filled it up and got it all ready, I told him I'd do it with him. I was skeptical, but I wanted to support him.

And let me tell you—it was horrific. I panicked. I couldn't breathe. I saw black spots. It was just as terrible as, if not more than, I had imagined. (I'm sure I'm really selling it for you right now!)

But then when I got out, and I started to warm up, I felt completely rejuvenated. It was almost like it shocked my body. My brain felt clear, my emotions felt stable, and that night, I'd never slept so soundly.

The results were worth the pain.

And now, it's like my body craves it. I hate doing it—it still is just as awful as day one. But I tell myself it's only for three minutes—three minutes in a twenty-four-hour day. That's doable.

The cold plunge is the perfect metaphor for life.

See, I am a woman who loves comfort. It's one of my goals in life. To have a welcoming home with a comfortable large couch that anyone can come sit on and not want to leave. If I find an outfit that feels like pajamas, I am winning. I love warm, steamy cups of coffee (with lots of cinnamon-roll creamer), nights spent around a glowing fire with friends, cuddling in my bed with a good book, and blankets. Any blankets. I almost always travel with my favorite blanket so I can be assured of something to cuddle with no matter where I land.

I love to be comfortable. The problem occurs when my love of comfort becomes an expectation and collides with my real life. When I love being comfortable not just physically, but internally as well, I start to lose sight of why I'm actually here.

God in His kindness gives us good things in life that are a gift. A hot shower, laughter with friends, a home-cooked meal, a rare find at an antique shop, movie night with your family, a local coffee shop that you may or may not frequent every other day because the homemade bread keeps calling your name. (I may or may not have gained the freshman fifteen while writing this book because, y'all, the bread at this local coffee shop!)

These are wonderful. And it's important to find delight in our lives—to play, to laugh, to make memories.

However, even though God tells us to do everything with thanksgiving, and we are to delight and have great gratitude for our lives, often our circumstances are not all fun or delightful. They are uncomfortable.

Every day we come up against trials, frustrations, irritations, things that trigger us and cause pain and hurt.

Our dishwasher breaks, and we won't get paid for another two weeks. *I had no idea how stressful finances would be.*

We have a long, hard day at work, and it seems like we are living for the weekend to come. *I had no idea work would be so demanding.*

We get in a fight with our spouse and go to sleep with our backs turned toward one another, silently choking back tears from the argument. *I had no idea marriage would feel so lonely.*

We spent hours today disciplining one of our kids. Hurtful words were spoken, so many tears were shed, and we lost our patience and were so ashamed of our anger. *I had no idea parenting would reveal my shadow side so vividly and I'd be fighting shame so much.*

So we try to numb the pain, try to grasp for some kind of happiness, some kind of distraction, some kind of ease, by turning to things we think will comfort us.

We start to drink a glass of wine at dinner every night as a treat, but before long it becomes a crutch. We can't wait until it's "five o'clock somewhere," and start counting down the hours until we can get home and drink that glass, which becomes that bottle, every night.

We lie in bed at night scrolling on Amazon, adding things to our cart, looking to shopping for our hit of happiness.

We escape into our favorite novel, because if we can't feel pursued in real life, at least we can read about the fantasy in hidden pages.

We binge-watch our favorite shows every night as our way to wind down, finding escape in stories that are not our own.

We scroll mindlessly through social media, looking at everyone's highlights, seeing beautiful photos and beautifully designed homes, looking for hope that our own lives can look and be just as beautiful as these photos. *I just need to try more. Do more.*

We take a little stimulant just to calm us down. It seems to be the only thing that calms our anxiety, that stops our physical pain for a small stint.

Life is harder than we expected it to be. We feel emptier than we ever thought possible. Our limitations are more glaring than we ever dreamed, and yet we live in an age where we're told that women have no limitations.

If being in control is an illusion, then at least we can be comfortable.

But the reality is, we have to get uncomfortable to find comfort.

God did not give us life so we could be comfortable; rather, He gave us life so we can be in an intimate relationship with Him, connected to Him, and so we can partner with Him to defeat darkness.

Our lives are not meant to be full of ease and free from pain.

I'm so thankful to live in America where we have running water and indoor toilets and heat that runs through our homes in the winter. (It gets cold even in Hawaii!) We can get groceries delivered to our house two hours after I place my order. I'm thankful for cars that get us all around the island. I love cuddling with my husband at night in our cozy bed and watching our favorite shows while we eat peanut butter cups and popcorn.

But how often do we long for those moments? How often do we live for those moments and try to just brace for the rest of life?

Americans are so comfortable. We have traded adventure for comfort. We have traded risk for ease. We have traded solitude for distraction. We have traded silence for constant noise.

I mean, you can place an Amazon order, and if you live near a store, it's delivered to your doorstep within the hour! We work out at gyms that are pumping AC. Our smartphones are with us every moment of every day, where we can, with the swipe of a finger, feel "connected" or "not bored" by checking our emails, scrolling IG, or shopping.

But the unfortunate thing that so many of us Americans have lost today is the reality of living uncomfortably.

Michael Easter in *The Comfort Crisis* diagnoses Americans by saying this: "We are living progressively sheltered, sterile, temperature-controlled, overfed, underchallenged, safety-netted lives. And it's limiting the degree to which we experience our 'one wild and precious life,' as poet Mary Oliver put it."[1]

The truth is, we can survive without being challenged. But is that what we really want? To survive? Don't we want more than that? Aren't we made for more than survival?

Dr. Marcus Elliott is a Harvard-trained physician who popularized an old Japanese purification ritual called *misogi* in which you take on challenges that radically expand your sense of what's possible. Mark Seery, a PhD who has done a lot of research on comfort zones, calls it "toughening."[2] Douglas Fields, one of the nation's leading neuroscientists, affirmed misogi and said, "When you undergo a new, stressful experience like misogi, you're transferring short term memories into long term memories—what just happened to you and what it led to, and what you should do next time you face a similar situation. 'In general, this is because memory is about the future. We retain experiences that may be of survival value at another time…this toughening process should give me this internal capacity that leaves me better able to deal with many things.'"³

Toughening. I'm constantly telling the kids, "We can do hard things." Hard things are not something to run from, but rather they are a gift for us to walk through and grow in. Yes, they are the last things we would choose, and they are difficult. But the results make the hard worth it. Knowing you can walk through something hard and be okay creates in us an inner strength and hope and resilience that cannot be made any other way.

For instance, the cold plunge. Yes, this seems a bit frivolous in light of the hard trials we walk through in life, but it applies. Submerging my body in forty-five-degree water for three minutes is my idea of hell. It's awful. It's not enjoyable, and honestly, it doesn't get easier. It hurts. I can't talk while I do it. The only thing I can do is focus on my breathing, and once in a blue moon recite a verse. It's incredibly stressful for my body. But then my timer goes off (sweet freedom!), I dunk my head (because why not end with the worst part?), and as I get out and then shiver under my towel, my brain fog disappears, and I feel peace. Warmth running through my body. I feel stronger. I feel clearer. And honestly, I feel like I'm much more emotionally stable to meet the demands of my day. I'm more mentally focused for my studies and writing.

Essentially, as I plunge, I am training my body and brain to do hard things, and when I do them, I am not only okay, but better for it, so when I meet the challenges of my day, I can face them better. Toughening, although not what we would choose, is actually a gift for our spiritual formation.

So when we feel tempted to not walk through the toughening, to avoid it at all costs, and when we are trying to grasp for comfort of all kinds, it's important to take note of what's behind the longing to be comfortable. Who or what you go to to find comfort reveals what is going on in your heart, and who you are trusting.

The enemy wants to numb us out, to distract us, to whisper hope in mirages that will only keep us sedated, settled, and asleep to our lives.

And God wants to wake us up! He wants to wake us up to His presence, His care and compassion, His love and grace.

He wants to give us real hope.

But we can only receive His real hope when we are real and honest about that which makes us feel uncomfortable. The things that keep us up at night, the fears that cycle through our minds, the anxieties that make our heart race, the emotions we carry deep inside of us.

In order to find true hope, we have to get uncomfortable.

God made us for resilient joy and abundant life, and He made us deeply emotional. This is not bad. Our emotions are what open up our hearts. The question is what do you do with them?

If we continue to stuff our feelings, to put on a facade that everything is okay, to push our feelings to the side because we think they are an inconvenience to the work before us, we miss out on the deep joy He wants to offer us. We mustn't choose ease anymore. Ease is a ploy that promises good but, in fact, causes us to miss out entirely on what God has for us and what He wants to do in and through us.

The trials, frustrations, and hardships of our lives—the ones that we wish weren't there and try to ignore or cover by fixing or managing—are actually "toughening" us. When we put them into the hands of God, when we are awake to all that He is wanting to do in and through us, we are becoming more and more like Him.

Romans 5:3–5 says, "Not only that, but we rejoice in our sufferings, knowing that suffering produces endurance, and endurance produces character, and character produces hope, and hope does not put us to shame, because God's love has been poured into our hearts through the Holy Spirit who has been given to us."

The answers to your discomforts in life are not found in the comforts of this world, but rather in the safety of God's heart.

He is your refuge.

He is your haven.

He is your strong tower.

You are not a burden to Him, but rather He delights in caring for you. He is Savior, but in order for Him to be Savior, we have to acknowledge that we need help every day. We need to abide in His presence, to find consolation in the only One who can truly console our hurting, broken, fragile hearts.

Jesus came to give us true life, true peace, and everlasting joy, but in what context? In a life full of ease and comfort? No. It's a life full of trials, pain, and growth. But we can be full of joy because of Jesus and have peace because of Jesus.

Yes, we have moments of peace and joy. When you beat your husband at pickleball (yes, I would like to officially write this here so it can be forever commemorated that I, Alyssa Bethke, have beaten Jeff Bethke at pickleball), when you and your best friend can't stop your giggles late at night, when your son tells you, "Mom, you're the best mom ever. I love you with my whole heart," when you catch a sunset or bite into a warm, buttery croissant, these are moments of wonder. Of joy.

But let me tell you this: your life is made for so much more than comfort. We need to wake up. To be awake to our hearts. Awake to our needs. Awake to others' hearts and needs. To be awake to what God is up to and to ask how we can join in.

Are you willing to step out? To say yes to God, whatever He may ask of you, whatever the future holds, knowing that His way is better and that He will be with you every step of the way? His love never leaves you. He just keeps getting closer.

There is a spiritual battle going on all around us, and we have to wake up to see it. We don't have to be afraid of it, but we need to take a stand and armor up and go to battle. You are needed on the team. We need you in the battle. You are made for the purposes of the kingdom of God, not for the kingdom of earth. Your life is more than having a nice house, a loving marriage with two kids, and looking twenty years younger than you really are. It's about more than being financially stable, being successful or having a big platform, or even being well-adjusted. It's more than having cute clothes, or climbing the ladder, or being well-liked.

What is your unique contribution that God has set you here for? You are needed—your voice, your care, your thoughtfulness, your presence. But if we are trying to live lives that are comfortable, we will miss it. We will be asleep to it.

The problem is we get comfort confused with living a well-ordered life. God did not come to give us comfortable lives, but He does want to give us well-ordered inner lives. He wants us to be self-aware, to bring Him our wounds and concerns and anxieties and fears, and to meet Him in that place. He knows we can't sort through all of that on our own, so He gives us His Holy Spirit to help, to lead and teach us, and other believers to speak into our lives and help us make sense out of all that leaves us tangled up inside. We're not called to comfort, but to be well-ordered is a high calling.

Augustine said, "To have a well-ordered heart is to love the right thing to the right degree in the right way with the right kind of love."[4]

The world's answer to a well-ordered inner life is balance, especially for women. We can do it all, be it all if we simply can balance it all. Time management, planners, schedules, to-do lists are our best friends. We are limitless, so we don't need to say no to anything; we simply need to know how to balance everything. Often, the world will tell us that a balanced life is a busy life, in which we can do it all in a way that makes others want to be just like us.

Never needing help is a badge of honor in our culture.

But the reality is that trying to balance it all is another way we try to assert control when life feels out of our control. It's another way we try to be God. It is a protection mechanism so we can feel like our lives are at ease, and everyone around us is eased.

John Ortberg has this amazing quote about the myth of balance in his book *The Life You've Always Wanted*:

The paradigm of balance simply doesn't capture the sense of compelling urgency worthy of human devotion. It is largely a middle-class pursuit. It lacks a notion that my life is to be given to something larger than myself. It lacks a call to sacrifice and self-denial, the wild, risky, costly, adventurous abandon of following Jesus. Ask hungry children in Somalia if they want to help you achieve balance, and you'll discover that they're hoping for something more from you. And I believe that deep down you are hoping for something more for you.[5]

You won't find the comfort and ease you're looking for in trying to balance it all. Balance won't bring the purpose or meaning you are looking for. It won't heal the hurts that you are holding. We look to it as the Band-Aid to our questions of whether we're worth it and whether we're enough. But there's so much more.

When you think of your favorite heroes, the saints that have gone before, you never think, *Wow, they just lived such balanced lives. How can I be more like them?* No! We think of how they gave it all, they sacrificed everything, they devoted their lives fully to all that is good, and even though they suffered, they made it through, stronger than before.

The midwives of Egypt feared God and didn't kill the male babies as Pharaoh had commanded, sacrificing their reputation and livelihood to save the Israelite children. Rahab protected the spies of Israel at the risk of her own life. David wandered in the wilderness for ten to fifteen years, running for his life from his father-in-law, Saul. Jesus went into the Garden of Gethsemane to cry it out with God. The apostles preached the good news and were imprisoned, beaten, martyred, sent to an island in total isolation. The spiritual father and mothers in the third century left their cities to live in the deserts of Egypt.

Paul says in 2 Corinthians 11:24–26,

Five times I received at the hands of the Jews the forty lashes less one. Three times I was beaten with rods. Once I was stoned. Three times I was shipwrecked; a night and a day I was adrift at sea; on frequent journeys, in danger from rivers, danger from robbers, danger from my own people, danger from Gentiles, danger in the city, danger in the wilderness, danger at sea, danger from false brothers…

These men and women of the faith did not run from the uncomfortable but fully said yes to whatever God asked them to do. They were all in, no matter the cost. These men and women risked it all to know God and to give His good news away.

But before they could give Him away, they spent time alone with Him. Moses was alone for forty days on a mountain. David was alone for ten to fifteen years in caves. Jesus was alone for forty days in the wilderness. John was alone on an island in his last days and wrote the book of Revelation.

I love this verse in Acts 4: "Now when they saw the boldness of Peter and John, and perceived that they were uneducated, common men, they were astonished. And they recognized that they had been with Jesus" (v. 13).

When we spend time with Jesus—not just reading Scripture, but letting Scripture seep into our hearts and minds, talking with God, telling Him our pains and thoughts and fears, seeing what He wants to tell us and what He wants to give us each day—not only will we be transformed, but people will see that we have been with Jesus.

And then only after being with God are we ready to go out. You are meant to partner with God. To look for where He is working, what He is up to, and to join Him. To give your very precious life away. Boldly.

I think we're so afraid of giving our lives away. We fear the cost. We fear the unknown. We fear what may be asked of us. Can we do it? Our American lives have conditioned us to be comfortable at whatever the cost. But do we realize what that costs our soul?

Do we truly believe that we follow and serve a good King? A King who cares for us, is with us, and loves us?

He invites us to get uncomfortable so that we can radiate His glory. To get uncomfortable in our inner lives so we can be healed and free. To get uncomfortable in our everyday lives so we can join Him in His mission, bringing hope and healing to the world and to those around us. The enemy wants to keep you hidden so God's light cannot penetrate the darkness. But friend, you are meant to shine. You are meant to step out into the dark so you can create atmospheres of His healing presence.

In the name of Jesus, let your fears be brought to His feet. In the name of Jesus, renounce comfort so you can live with fullness. Fullness comes as we empty ourselves of our fears and worries and learn to live with a hearty YES.

Lord, anything. And everything. I give it all to you. Whatever the cost. Whatever the call. Whatever the discomfort. Anything.

Because He is a good God. A good Father. A good King. We can entrust our lives to Him, the One who comforts us as we walk through the uncomfortable. The One who has far more for us than we could ever think or imagine. But we have to get rid of the things that block His Holy Spirit from moving and working in us. He wants to be like living water and move through us, constantly flowing like a river.

Will you say yes to Him? Will you relinquish your tight grip on your life, your fear of all that is out of your control, the fear of letting people down, of letting balls drop, of not being able to hold it all together?

And trust that He goes before you, and He holds all things together, and you can take the light way of saying yes to His great adventure?

Spiritual Practice

Ask the Lord, "Are there any areas of my life that I'm afraid to 'go there' because they're uncomfortable? Are there any places where I'm holding back?"

Sit there for a few moments and catch the first thing that comes to your mind. Then pray and ask God to give you the courage to go there. To not let fear stop you any longer.

And ask Him, "What do You want me to do with that?"

See what He says. Your yes is your gateway to freedom.

PART III

LOSING HEART

We've seen how we can neglect our hearts by stuffing our emotions and scooting matters of the heart aside. It's easier to focus on our strong desires rather than our deepest ones.

Another way we deal with the matters of our hearts is by trying to gain strength of heart by doing whatever we can to look good, be good, and have ease. We've seen that although we are called for a great purpose, we are not what we do. We are not responsible for managing the outcomes of life. We cannot control the people around us or our circumstances so that they go the way we want. We cannot change people, and we cannot change their perception of us. We cannot insulate our lives in such a way that we are protected from the uncomfortable and the painful. We are called for so much more. We are called to open up our hearts to God, and we find that in the risk, we are secure.

This next section then moves into how we can care for our hearts and have hope in the midst of broken ideals, great disappointments, and deep griefs. How can we come to God in the moments when we are doubting His goodness? Who are we when everything seems to shatter before our eyes? What does God have for us then?

8

DEALING WITH DISAPPOINTMENTS

There are two types of people in life:

The kind who watch movies to escape their realities.

And the kind who watch movies to enter into reality.

I am the former.

I love a good movie, a good TV show that is happy, funny, and has a feel-good ending. I think that's why I loved all the Disney princess movies as a little girl, because the prince and princess always end up together and "live happily ever after" despite the odds, despite the evil villain or the different class structures. *Hart of Dixie* is my favorite show of all time because Zoe Hart makes me laugh, and you know that at the end of the show, even with their differences and the love triangle and the Bluebell mean girls, the town will end up rooting for each other and all come together under that white gazebo in song and dance.

Jeff will watch all those shows with me, but he would much prefer a movie full of drama, intrigue, and mystery. He likes a movie better if it doesn't end all wrapped up in a nice bow, because it's more *realistic*.

Now, regardless of what type of movie watcher you are, I believe we all have lots of ideals that we hope for in life so we can all "live happily ever after." The *Merriam-Webster.com Dictionary* defines *ideal* as "a standard of perfection, beauty, or excellence."[1]

Ideals are how we expect life will go. They're the dreams we have for how things will play out or how they should look or what they should be like. They can be expectations that we put on ourselves or that someone else gives us. They can be long-held dreams and hopes, like becoming a mother, or they can be more day-to-day, but they're standards of what we think life should look like.

Although our ideals can help us have vision, they often cause pressure, stress, and anxiety.

Perfect home.

Perfect youth.

Perfect body.

Perfect mom (or wife, friend, sister, or daughter).

Perfect worker.

Perfect life.

The problem is that I think we as women start with good ideals, but they often get broken with comparison and end in frustration.

For instance, here are some of the things I idealize:

1. A perfect home that is beautiful with no mess that's totally organized and looks like a Studio McGee spec home. (I sometimes secretly want to be Shea McGee.) *But the reality is that I live in my home, with four other people and two dogs, on a budget, and these people like to eat, play, and work in that home.*

2. Everlasting youth and beauty from my twenties. I pluck at least two gray hairs off my head weekly, have wrinkles forming around my eyes and in between my brows, and have more conversations with my girlfriends about Botox than I'd ever expect. *The reality is that I'm aging, and I'm longing to look youthful*

because I'm not quite sure how to age beautifully. Is beauty in my past?

3. A perfect body but end up: having an internal battle in my mind wishing I were smaller here, thinner there, stronger here. *Because the truth is I still am battling what I think a woman should look like, what I should look like, but my body is changing and I'm having to accept this thirty-six-year-old body in new ways.*

4. Being a perfect mom who can turn any birthday party into the party of the year with my balloon-arch capabilities and my cake-baking skills. *However, I live a full life and although I make it a priority to celebrate my people, I also tend to stay up until midnight the night before, putting together birthday presents that are far larger than I thought when I bought them and take way longer to assemble (have mercy) because I'm not that organized or that detailed.*

5. Being perfectly capable with no limitations where I can go through my day checking off all my to-dos because "Look at me! I am Miss Productivity! I can get it done! I can conquer the world!" Just watch out, everyone who I meet today. *Because the truth is that often I make my day more about the task than the people, and that just hurts all of us.*

6. An exciting and fulfilled life that looks as beautiful and adventurous and fun as those of other people I follow on IG. *But the reality is I'm only seeing a small percentage of their lives, and although I'm so happy for them, and it inspires me, sometimes it leaves me feeling less than, or wishing for a different season than the one I'm in. And truth be told, sometimes jealousy takes root in my heart when my life does not look like theirs.*

I know that we know these are all ideals that are not reality. But it often doesn't stop us from reaching for them. How many nights do we lie in bed scrolling through Pinterest or Instagram, longing and wishing for our lives to look like *that*? How many times have we made the to-do lists, the goal lists, of how to attain *that*? And if we're honest with ourselves, we can all see how those come from comparison, from longing for what someone else has or is because we think that will make us happier. That is what we're missing. That is the goal. But it only leaves us feeling frustrated, defeated, less than.

Our ideals leave us feeling exhausted. They leave us weary from the pressure. They leave us unraveling because our lives don't look like that.

The truth is those ideals need to be thrown out. We need to take seriously the fact that comparison only leads to despair. When these ideals don't play out the way we want, the way we hope, and the way we try, we can tend to respond in shame.

I'm not good enough. I should be so much more. I am a failure. I can't get it together.

"Comparison is the thief of obedience and joy," says my friend Emily Jamieson. It robs us of obeying the Lord in the life that He has given each one of us, and it robs us of the joy that He gives.

Our lives are so much more than looking like a beautiful Pinterest ad. They are so much more than what we can boast about on IG. What matters is what's going on inside our home, not what it looks like. Is it a peaceful place full of love and grace as we welcome the Spirit to reside there? And no, this doesn't mean no one ever sins or screams or slams doors. It just means that when we do, is there forgiveness, is there honesty, is there grace? Is there a seeking to be known and to know?

What matters is if we radiate the love of Jesus, if we celebrate our people well, if we care for our bodies and move them, if we say yes to the tasks that Jesus gives us each day regardless of what they look like on paper. What matters is if we can truly receive our lives with joy and hope, whatever season we are in.

So many of our ideals are so much deeper than they appear at first, and there are often very deep reasons we hold to them. It's not just that we want life to appear beautiful and breezy and perfect. I truly want to have deep, godly desires, but the problem is that I think they need to play out the way I think is best. For instance, take marriage. Marriage is a good, godly desire. But before I was married, I thought marriage would be an ongoing romantic comedy where despite the long days and perhaps financial struggles, we would always choose each other and fall asleep cuddling. I thought Jeff would relate to me the way I relate to him. I thought he would need the same things I need. Honestly, I thought it'd be so much easier than it is. I didn't anticipate our shadow sides, the areas where we carry baggage into our marriage, the areas that still need healing and freedom. And I didn't anticipate that the areas that are the hardest are actually the very areas that God is using to form us into His likeness. We are getting to see each other become our glorified selves. It's not what I thought—in fact, it's so much harder—but it's also so much richer.

I had also idealized motherhood. I thought motherhood would look like cute organic baby clothes and tons of cuddles and crafts and laughter and kids running through our house with joy and a white minivan where we'd make memories together as we explored and lived and learned. My kids are the most amazing miracles and gifts, but motherhood is beyond stretching. I had no idea how selfish, angry, and impatient I was! (Ha!) I did not take into account hearts and development and grace upon grace upon grace. I didn't anticipate the hardships of discipleship and raising world changers that have their own opinions and big emotions and wills. But motherhood for me is what God is using to make me more and more like Him as I constantly learn to be present, to love well, to pour out all that I have while also trusting that God alone can do the work in them. It is making me stronger, more hopeful, more patient, more loving, and more resilient. And I am reminded daily that although it's not what I thought, it is one of the richest gifts in my life.

I thought ministry and work would be exciting and adventurous and glorious all the time. And although I love what I do—it is where my heart leaps with joy over learning about and giving away Jesus—it is so much harder than I ever thought. I did not anticipate the spiritual battle that comes along with it. I did not anticipate my weaknesses, limitations, and insecurities. I did not anticipate the hardships; I simply didn't factor those in.

So yes, I have ideals that include a perfectly clean home, but I also have ideals about how my life should play out and how things should look, and I am learning how my ideals are not so ideal because they actually prohibit me from receiving the deeper gifts God has for me.

It goes back to ease and approval and control. I don't want to feel pain. I don't want to have hard. I want to "mount up wings like eagles!" (Is. 40:31) So I imagine a life of ideals, when God is inviting me to have the imagination of heaven.

Our lives are not a Disney movie; rather, they are a battlefield. We are at war. There is a complex battle of wills taking place— God, Satan, and people's. God has a will, but He doesn't push it so far that we don't have choice.

Let's look at some of the saints of the Bible, some who are found in Hebrews 11. We see saints who did see God's promise come to fruition, but not in full. A yes, and not yet. Sarah giving birth in her old age and yet not living long enough to see her legacy. Moses leading the Israelites out of captivity but not being able to enter the promised land because of his sin. The prophets crying out for a different vision and reformation, and yet never seeing the vision come to be. Jeremiah and Isaiah were exiled, and had to trust that God would rescue His people in another generation. John the Baptist preparing the way for the Messiah, and knowing Jesus, and yet dying before he saw the Kingdom inaugurated. We hear of those who "through faith conquered kingdoms, enforced justice, obtained promises, stopped the mouths of lions, quenched the power of fire, escaped the edge of the sword, were made strong out of weakness, became mighty in war, put foreign armies to flight. Women received back their dead by resurrection" (vv. 33–35). But none of these people got to see Jesus.

We also see great suffering from those who have been with Jesus: "Some were tortured, refusing to accept release, so that they might rise again to a better life. Others suffered mocking and flogging, and even chains and imprisonment. They were stoned, they were sawn in two, they were killed with the sword. They went about in skins of sheep and goats, destitute, afflicted, mistreated" (vv. 35–37).

And you know what the author of Hebrews says about all of these men and women of faith who did not get to see the promise fulfilled?

"Of whom the world was not worthy."

I get chills when I read this line. Why do I spend so much time and energy trying to get my worth or comfort from the world? We are in this world but not of it. There is so much more.

Hebrews 12:1–2 goes on to say,

> Therefore, since we are surrounded by so great a cloud of witnesses, let us also lay aside every weight, and sin which clings so closely, and let us run with endurance the race that is set before

us, looking to Jesus, the founder and perfecter of our faith, who for the joy that was set before him endured the cross, despising the shame, and is seated at the right hand of the throne of God.

We are in a race, and sometimes the journey gets heavy. God is inviting us to throw off all the weight, all the heavy burdens—the ideals, the performance, the trying to manage and control how things turn out—and look to Him. Look to the One who ran the race, endured such pain and agony, and all in joy. You were His joy. You were the reason. He is the One we look to and run with and run for. It's not about our ideals, but rather it's about meeting God in the midst of the broken ideals and finding Him to be more precious and desirable than what we thought life should look like.

Even when our circumstances don't play out the way we thought they would, God is faithful to change us, if we allow Him. He is the God of restoration, of repair, and He will make our pain worthwhile. He is actually doing a beautiful work in us when life around us feels ugly.

Romans 8:28 (AMP) says, "And we know [with great confidence] that God [who is deeply concerned about us] causes all things to work together [as a plan] for good for those who love God, to those who are called according to His plan *and* purpose."

In God's hands, our broken ideals are actually caverns for the love of God, who works it out for our good. For our becoming more like Him. God can make our hopeless ideals into a hope-filled reality when surrendered in the hands of love,

Counselor and author Larry Crabb says, "Maybe there is not a shortcut to joy. Maybe God sometimes frustrates our desire to experience Him in order to deepen it."[2]

God sometimes allows for the stripping of the things we've idealized to give us an even better ideal. He is wanting to purify our ideals to give us Himself. My counselor poignantly said to me once, "God is supremely ideal. He's not chastising our idealism. He's freeing our ideals."

Larry Crabb gives us this vision: "The highest dream we could ever dream, the wish that if granted would make us happier than any other blessing, is to know God, to actually experience Him."[3]

I was talking with my friend Sara the other day, really blubbering to her and barely able to get my words out as I honestly shared about a deep pain in my life. An area that leaves me feeling alone and defeated and wondering, *How much longer, Lord? Will it always be like this?*

And as much as I long for it to change, for healing, for a breakthrough, you know what she said?

She said, "Alyssa, I know it's not easy and it can be unbelievably painful, but you need to get to a place where you can fully accept that if this never changes, if this circumstance stays this way forever, you will be okay. You can still live with hope and joy and peace, knowing that God is good and you have God."

We cannot do this alone. This is done with community, as you walk with others that can hope for you and with you and can come alongside you and process. It's not a fast thing, a forced thing, but rather it's a journey of crying out to God, of being honest with Him, of opening your heart to Him over and over and over and finding that He meets you with His steadfast love that will soothe and heal and strengthen your weary and exhausted soul. It's learning to come, and come again, to the Father's arms. It's a slow and gentle journey that cannot be snapped together, demanded to change or fixed with a five-step plan.

This is sturdiness of soul. This is the life that we are invited into. Not that we aren't bothered by pain, or that we don't grieve and have sorrow, or that we don't face disappointment when the things we've idealized don't look like we thought they would. But it means that in the very areas where we feel like life has fallen apart, that we have fallen apart, where the longings don't come to fruition and the dreams lie broken on the ground, we are still okay and, in fact, good. Not good in the Miley Cyrus way, where she can buy herself flowers and doesn't need anyone and isn't touched by loneliness, but in the way where we can still be whole and full and have our feet firmly planted on the ground in the midst of the barrenness and burdens of life.

Sara spoke that truth—of getting to a place of complete surrender and being securely grounded in the "if it doesn't change," not because it's not possible, but because it is. Because God is so rich in love, so full of mercy and compassion, so tender and present and gracious, that He can fill every crevice of our soul and heal us and give us such great hope.

Lamentations 3:22–24:

The steadfast love of the LORD never ceases;
his mercies never come to an end;
they are new every morning;
great is your faithfulness.
"The LORD is my portion," says my soul,
"therefore I will hope in him."

The abundant life does not mean we get all the things we want, but it means that we get all of God. His fullness. And even better, we get all of His fullness in the midst of the emptiness of life. We get all of Him when everything seems to be sucked out of us and stripped away from us.

And He's actually enough.

But the path that takes that truth from our head to our hearts is often through the dark valleys of life.

My friend Emilie often will say to me, "'What if' becomes our 'even if.'"

There can be so many what-ifs, whether they are in our worrisome minds or in our actual lives. It can become crippling if we let our minds sit on them for too long.

Isaiah 43:2 says, "When you pass through the waters, I will be with you; and through the rivers, they shall not overwhelm you; when you walk through fire you shall not be burned, and the flame shall not consume you."

Notice here that it says *when* you go through these things, not *if* you go through these things. They will come. And what does Isaiah say? God will still be with us. He will not let them overwhelm you and you will not be burned; you won't be consumed. Even if, God is good and will be with you and in you and sustain you.

God wants to take our *what-ifs* and move us to *even if.*

Even if I never marry.

Even if I'm never close to my parents.

Even if my autoimmune disease never changes.

Even if my husband never comes around.

Even if the diagnosis isn't good.

Even if I lose my job.

Even if…God is still good to me. God is my greatest joy. God will never leave me or forsake me. God holds all my tears. God will strengthen me and fill me.

What if the promise isn't that the pain is taken away, but that Jesus increases our capacity in the midst of the pain? He increases our capacity for more of Himself. For more of His power. For more of His hope.

It's as we're emptied that we can be full of Him. And the fullness of Him is the glory of God and the goodness of mankind.

Spiritual Practice

Take out a piece of paper and write your what-ifs down. Bullet-list them.

Then go through and write "even if" next to them. Work through your fears. And push yourself to see God there, even in the "even if."

Is God sufficient for you?

9

DISMANTLED DREAMS

We were in Vermont for the fall. We arrived at the end of summer so we could soak up the last hot days of jumping in the river and picking blackberries before it quickly faded into autumn, where the oak trees get lit on fire, turning yellow and orange and red. Apple cider donuts. Maple syrup ice cream. Maple syrup pizza. Maple syrup everything! Walks through the forest, feeding the animals, notebooking about mushrooms and acorns and squirrels. It was the greatest fall with the family. Autumn on the farm in Vermont was pure magic. I was living all my Gilmore Girl dreams. We were there to host retreats—Jeff hosting them for teachers, writers, and men and I was hosting one for women. It was glorious.

And yet, I came with a broken heart. A weary spirit. The loss of friendships had been so crushing, starting homeschool again after such a hard year was daunting, and anticipating being alone a lot while Jeff worked most of the retreats felt scary.

I was changing and growing and being made strong, but I was smack-dab in my heartache and weariness.

And during those first couple of weeks, it seemed like Jeff and I couldn't stop butting heads. Really, so much of it was because of the fear I was carrying. I feared being alone—not just physically, but emotionally. This was go time for Jeff, and we already were coming into it not as connected as I'd wanted. The year had proven to be challenging with his health. He had been so sick for months, going to doctor after doctor, but no one was able to figure out what was wrong. Depression set in, as is common when you are chronically ill and have no energy for life. Although he was feeling better for a short time, it had taken a toll on our marriage. We were coming up on our tenth wedding anniversary, but instead of feeling lovey-dovey, I was feeling detached.

My mentor Tammy came for a visit to the farm to help lead one of the retreats. She and I were staying in the same house (the kids and Jeff were off-site while I led the women's retreat), and before the retreat started, she came out of her room, and as we passed each other in the hallway, she looked me in the eyes and said, "Alyssa, how are you and Jeff?"

Her questions always seem to be arrows pointing to my deepest needs.

Tears welled up in my eyes. I couldn't speak for a moment. Because, you see, I was leading this retreat out of my complete brokenness and was already doing what I could to hold it all together. To be able to show up to serve and love and lead. But how do you do that when you feel as though your own heart is in pieces?

We went into my room and sat down on my bed, and I told her my true heart about how our marriage was, and how I was so sad, so discouraged and disappointed. How I desperately longed for intimacy, for unity, for connection, but how it was so hard in this season.

She held me, and then she led me through an imaginative prayer. I've learned over the last few years how our imaginations are a gift from God and that they can help us hear from God as we use them to see colors, pictures, or simply what it's like to sit in the presence of Jesus. People use their imaginations every day to create artwork, stories, designs, food. They also use them for their demise. We must redeem our imaginations, and what a gift it is to use them to hear from God.

So we sat on my queen-size bed covered in an orange velvet quilt, while the sun started to set on the horizon, causing the light in my room to shift ever so slightly with its golden hour.

She held my hand and came before Jesus with me.

"Alyssa, I want you to imagine a safe place, whether it's real or imaginary, and then picture Jesus there," Tammy said. "Where is He? Is He sitting? Walking? Waiting? Take note of the time of day, your surroundings, how it feels to be in the presence of Jesus. Try to look Him in the eyes. What do you notice?"

I have done this before. It's one of my favorite things to do. Because Jesus is always with us, it's just a matter of us becoming awake to and aware of His presence.

"Now, I want you to tell Him your disappointments."

Through my running nose and with tears dripping off my face (it was a little bit of an ugly cry), I simply told Jesus my pain. How I so longed to be pursued, to be connected, to be closer. I told Him my disappointment with Jeff's sickness, how it broke my heart that he was in pain and that the doctors couldn't figure out what was going on. I confessed how I was operating out of fear and was scared I'd be alone for the fall. I confessed how I hadn't been as kind or humble or generous of heart, how I withheld love in some ways.

While I was praying, my hands were full of wet tissues. Scattered on the bed, scattered on the floor. I had let it all out.

"What would your pain look like if it were an object?"

"A handful of tissues. Wet. Crumpled."

"Okay, now give that handful of tissues to God and ask Him what He wants to give you in exchange."

And immediately I saw Jesus giving me a bouquet of hydrangeas. Full. Rich. Blooming.

"Lord, what do you want Alyssa to know?"

And I felt Him say (I don't audibly hear God's voice, but I can sense what He's speaking to my heart) that He was taking my sorrow and disappointment and exchanging it for beauty. He was my Husband, and He was after my heart. He was pursuing me.

For the next month, I clung to that vision and the truth that God was after my heart. I felt Him whisper to me every day to be with Him. I'd wake up early before the kids, brew a cup of coffee, and sit by the fireplace reading His words to me in His Word. I'd go for walks in the woods, talking with Him, telling Him all about my day. I'd sit out on the lawn while the kids biked around the farm, feeling His presence with me as I watercolored, as I simply looked at the trees slowly change colors.

He was pursuing me. And I was pursuing Him. I had never felt so connected with Him. In all my everyday, ordinary moments. It was like I was breathing in His presence, and I was not lonely.

Weeks later, Jeff and I were walking the streets of Woodstock, grabbing a coffee and looking at all the cute shops, when we passed this white house with columns and black shutters. There was a gardener out front trimming back all of the expansive hydrangea bushes. The ground lay covered with dried hydrangea stems, all in antique white and green colors.

"Sir, would it be possible to gather a few stems to take home?" I shyly asked.

"Oh, take as many as you want. I'm just going to throw them away."

I couldn't believe it. Hundreds of dried hydrangea blooms lay there waiting for me to take home. Even though they were no longer their glorious blues and pinks, they were even prettier with their antique tones. I grabbed an armful, unable to stop the smile that was sweeping across my face. Jeff said, "You're beaming!"

Hydrangeas are my absolute favorite. I grew up in Washington, and most people would have large blue hydrangea bushes in their yards. We had hydrangeas as the centerpieces at our wedding reception, and I've always dreamed of having a large walkway up to our front door that is lined with hydrangeas.

God had shown me a picture of a bouquet of hydrangeas, comforting my heart with His love and pursuit, and now I held in my arms a dozen of the largest hydrangea flowers I'd ever seen.

That fall proved to be one of the best in our marriage. Being away from our normal lives, just our family, and having time to connect and be together was so healing. We had hours of conversations, of walking the forest together, of sitting around the campfire at night processing together, of serving together those who came on the retreats. It was beautiful.

But even more so, I felt the Lord's loving pursuit of my heart all fall. It was as if He kept beckoning my heart: "Alyssa, come away with Me. Walk with Me. I'll show you how."

Throughout the weeks as I strolled through that dense forest with the light beaming through the yellow leaves, the dusty path below my feet, the squirrels racing up the tree trunks, I had hours to talk to Him. Hours to listen. I would tell Him what I was feeling, tell Him my questions, concerns, my desires, my longings. I would listen for what He wanted me to know, what truth He wanted to give me.

I was what the Japanese call "forest bathing." This activity has become popularized in the last few years in our world where we are so attached to our phones and spend most of our time indoors. Studies show that when we walk in nature—whether it's in a park or a forest—detached from our phones for just ten to twenty minutes, it does a world of good for our bodies, stress levels, immunity, and mind.

But even more, I was bathing in the presence of God. And what refreshment His presence brought. It was as if He were breathing new life into my deadened cells. Into the areas that felt worn-out, exhausted, so discouraged.

The problem I see with so many women today is that we live with disappointments, but we're not being honest about them. We either live hardened, unforgiving lives where bitterness takes root in our souls, or we try to suppress our disappointments because we don't know what to do with them. Shouldn't we be happy all the time? Content? Grateful? *What would others think if I actually said that my life is a disappointment?* Most of the time, it's not our whole lives that we're disappointed by, but a piece that plays a huge role in our inner lives. We can have small disappointments, like the barista making our coffee order wrong, or big, life-altering disappointments, like cancer or infertility, that leave us grappling with the goodness of God.

God, I thought I heard You promise me that I would have a child, and yet I still am barren.

I thought that friend would be a friend for life, and yet we don't talk anymore and I feel so lonely.

I started this ministry, and I thought it would be so fruitful, but it just keeps dwindling in numbers. Am I doing something wrong? Did I hear from God wrong?

I thought that if I took on this job, it would benefit me, but instead it is taking away my quality of life.

I planned this whole vacation and have been so desperate to get away, but it got cancelled because others got sick and couldn't go.

I keep putting myself out there and have been waiting for a godly man, but all my dates turn into a one-date dinner with no hope of a future.

We don't want to hear Christian clichés, and we truthfully don't know how God would respond, or if He'd respond at all, if we honestly told Him our disappointments. Would He care? Would He just expect us to trust Him? How do we grapple with life's disappointments and still trust in God's goodness and care?

The truth is, however, that life is full of disappointments. People disappoint us. Circumstances disappoint us. Weather disappoints us. We disappoint ourselves!

God doesn't expect us not to be disappointed.

He wants us to come to Him *in* our disappointment.

He wants us to come with honesty, telling Him openly and rawly how we feel, what questions we have, what's going on inside of our bodies.

Our disappointments are not meant to be stuffed down, but they are meant to be brought to the light and exchanged for hope.

And hope is not a feeling.

Hope is a person.

And hope, as one of my best friends Emilie reminds me, is not something we can see. It is in the darkness, it is in the impossible, it is when we can't see any way out, but we trust that God can do it. He can move. He is working even when we don't see it.

Hope is the light in the darkness. Oh, we can feel disappointed by God.

God, why did you not open that door for us to move there?

God, why was my baby born with this condition?

God, how could You let my dad get cancer?

God, why is this anxiety still crippling me?

God, why am I not healed?

The enemy wants to use your disappointment to put a wedge between you and God, and God invites you to come to Him with it. The enemy wants you to doubt God, to run away from God, to put up all your walls to protect yourself, or better yet, to cause you to not "go there" and just shut down. God wants to sit with you, listen to you, and give you the true hope that is found in His presence.

"Why are you cast down, O my soul, and why are you in turmoil within me? Hope in God; for I shall again praise Him, my salvation and my God" (Psalm 42:5–6).

Author and speaker Lysa TerKeurst says, "What if disappointment is really the exact appointment your soul needs to radically encounter God?"[1]

What if we saw disappointments as an invitation to sit with Jesus instead of an excuse to run away?

What if we held disappointments as an opportunity to be honest with ourselves about our expectations and our experiences, and bring them to God, instead of as a closed door to really living?

I think sometimes we fear how God will answer, if we'll be disappointed with God, or, worst of all, if He'll be disappointed with us.

"There is no fear in love, but perfect love casts out fear" (1 John 4:18). God is not only perfectly loving, but He is love Himself. If we truly understood that, we would not fear in His presence. We wouldn't fear His response; we wouldn't fear His thoughts or judgments. We would not fear the future either. Why? Because we would know that we know *that we know* that God loves us. Nothing can separate us from His love. There is no shame in perfect love. There is no need to run and hide. God is abundantly kind, overwhelmingly gracious; He is tender and gentle. He is full of compassion and mercy. Yes, He is just and will discipline us and convict us of sin, but even in that, it's done because He loves us, and it's done in His kindness. God can take your disappointment.

He wants you to entrust it to Him so He can mend your broken heart, but He cannot do His good work if you hide away in your disappointments.

God is after your heart. He wants all of you. He understands what disappointment is; oh, how many times did God's heart grieve over humanity? How many times did Jesus ache after the world? And truth be told, He disappointed a lot of people. The Israelites thought He was coming to defeat Roman rule, and yet He died on a humiliating cross. The disciples thought this was it, the Messiah had come, and yet He willingly went to the cross. He didn't come as a mighty ruler to defeat all the enemies, but rather, He laid down His life for all that were lost and needing a savior. And then three days later, He proved His promises were true. He proved His power. He proved His goodness.

I think of the story of Hannah in 1 Samuel 1. Hannah was married to a man named Elkanah, who deeply loved her, more than his other wife! (That's right. The Bible is wild with its real stories of real people.) However, there was a problem (other than the fact that her husband was married to another woman). Hannah could not get pregnant. For years, she longed to have a baby, to give Elkanah a son, to have a lineage, but she remained barren. Back in the ancient world, a woman's worth and purpose was in having children so the family lineage could carry on. Not having children could leave a wife vulnerable to divorce and abandonment, leaving her destitute.

Elkanah and his two wives, Hannah and Peninnah, would travel to Jerusalem every year to sacrifice to the Lord.

Now, imagine this. They're sitting around the table, and

when Elkanah sacrificed, he passed helpings from the sacrificial meal around to his wife Peninnah and all her children, but he always gave an especially generous helping to Hannah because he loved her so much, and because GOD had not given her children. But her rival wife taunted her cruelly, rubbing it in and never letting her forget that GOD had not given her children. This went on year after year. Every time she went to the sanctuary of GOD she could expect to be taunted. Hannah was reduced to tears and had no appetite. (1 Samuel 1:4–7 MSG)

Hannah was a woman of deep sorrow. Such disappointments in her life and circumstances. Can you imagine being described as a woman who was "reduced to tears and had no appetite"? Life had gone from her body. And not only did she remain longing, and sorrowful, but it was cruelly thrown in her face day to day.

But then listen what she does with her sorrow. With her disappointment.

"Then she pulled herself together, slipped away quietly, and entered the sanctuary" (v. 9 MSG).

She goes to be with God.

"Crushed in soul, Hannah prayed to GOD and cried and cried—inconsolably" (v. 10 MSG).

So much so that the priest Eli thought she was drunk.

She made a fool of herself to pray her heart out to God. She didn't hold back. She didn't nuance it or try to package it nicely. She laid it all out. She was gut-wrenchingly honest.

Hannah tells the priest, "I'm a woman brokenhearted. I haven't been drinking. Not a drop of wine or beer. The only thing I've been pouring out is my heart, pouring it out to GOD. Don't for a minute think I'm a bad woman. It's because I'm so desperately unhappy and in such pain that I've stayed here so long" (vv. 15–16 MSG).

Eli blesses her and sends her out, and it ends with saying Hannah "ate heartily, her face radiant" (v. 18 MSG).

Sometimes I think we worry that if we actually go to God in all honesty, we'll be spent, kept in ashes, rolling around in even more sorrow.

But the opposite is true.

When we go to God and lay it all down before Him, no matter how long or how many days it takes, not withholding anything, we will come away nourished, given a full appetite, and glowing with the radiance of His presence.

It's where God exchanges our sorrow for His joy. Our ashes for His beauty.

Even if our circumstances don't change, even if we have to face the hard road, we are not left empty-handed, but rather are given the goodness of God. We are given God Himself. We have God to hold on to, to cling to, to hide in.

Hannah was given her desire. But catch this—she was given a son, but she kept her promise of committing him to the Lord. When he was a young boy, she took him to the temple for Eli to raise so he could be a priest. God had his hand on Samuel and wanted to partner with him in great ways. And Hannah surrendered once again to the Lord. Giving up her son, letting someone else raise him, not having him at home to be an apprentice of his father, to carry on the family name. Her disappointment had turned to joy, but in that joy, she surrendered her son and entrusted him to someone else. What faith, what faithfulness, what trust.

Sometimes in our disappointments we can doubt God. I'm sure Hannah doubted God for years.

Why not me, God? Are you good? Are you withholding from me?

If your disappointments are leading to doubts, go to God. There is no doubt, no anger, no sadness that He cannot hold. He can take it. Hannah let herself look undignified before the Lord, and before the priest. Our sorrows, our disappointments are deep and sometimes guttural. In the presence of the Lord, you do not have to hold it together. You can let yourself unravel because He is the master of mending.

However, within the doubt, be careful to not glorify it. Don't stay in the doubt. Don't put a timeline on it, and don't pressure yourself to "get mended" in this way, at this time. But don't hold your doubt so tightly that it becomes part of your identity either. God longs for you to bring your doubt to Him so He can give you faith.

I think in our Christian circles the past few years, we have started to glorify our doubt. And on the one hand, we want to welcome people into the presence of God and bring their doubts there. There is no doubt God cannot face. He will meet you in your wrestling, but the doubts brought to God are meant to move you *through* to faith. Wrestle with your disappointments, bring them to God, but stay there, in the sanctuary, until you come to the breaking of the new day. Don't rush yourself in the sanctuary. Don't force yourself to dust yourself off and get up and go. Stay. Cry. Be honest. Morning will come, not according to you but rather to the One who holds the sun and moon in His hands.

God wants to meet you where your disappointments are. You may worry that He is not good when you look at your life, but I guarantee that when you go to the sanctuary and cry it all out, you will come away fully nourished and remembering who He is, what He's done, and what He promises to do. Your circumstances may not change, your disappointments may remain. But you will be strengthened, you will be met with hope and grace and will find a way to acceptance. But acceptance only comes as we go through the disappointment, not try to pass over it or pretend it's not there.

What if your disappointments are actually gifts in disguise?

What if they are to show you even greater desires? What if they are carving out places in you to be full of His delight?

Get honest with your disappointments. Sit with them, in God's presence. And see what He wants to give you in exchange.

Spiritual Practice

Are you holding on to a disappointment? Sit with God and bring it to Him. If it were an object, what would it be? What would it feel like? Now, picture yourself giving it over to God. What does He do with it? What does He give you in exchange?

Giving God our disappointments doesn't necessarily mean our circumstance will change, but it will release us from having it weigh us down.

10

GUT-HONEST GRIEF

It was the middle of the night in August when Jeff and I woke up to an alert on our phones. With one eye opened, I read the text but quickly put my phone back on my nightstand, not recognizing the names or understanding the message. A minute later, Jeff's phone rang. The honeymoon couple who were staying in our guest apartment were asking Jeff if we needed to evacuate.

He sat up, said he'd call them back, and quickly researched and found that the street names I'd been unable to recognize in that text were right by us, and we indeed did need to evacuate our home. He went outside to check on the fire.

The wind had been howling all night. We had lost power. I hadn't slept well.

I quickly got out of bed, curious what to do in a moment of crisis.

"Babe, you gotta come out here," Jeff said.

I stepped outside, and there, to the left of our property, was a huge orange cloud, billowing and expanding by the second.

We quickly (well, not as quickly as we could have, with trying to herd our three cats into our car; now I know why they say corralling your kids is like herding cats—almost impossible) loaded up our car and drove down the mountain. We traveled about forty-five minutes to a coffee shop that had opened at the crack of dawn. We ate. We waited. We tried to be normal for the kids, but really, I think I was just in denial of what was really happening.

Hours later, the fire by our house was more contained, but the historical town of Lahaina, on the other side of the island, was wiped away in a matter of two hours. Everything—homes, jobs, schools, boats, the harbor. The whole town. Gone.

The hurricane-force winds had blown down numerous power lines, which then set fire to the dry grasses, and it quickly all burned down. Families fled for their lives, but there was only one way out of the town, down a one-way road that traverses the back-side of the island.

Families and people fled to the ocean, with the fire sprinting and flying down the hill. They stayed there for hours, floating on any piece of trash or wood they could find, covering their faces and mouths from the expanding smoke.

In a matter of hours, our island of Maui was changed. Grief, devastation, utter shock swept through.

How could this possibly have happened?

Everyone, on Maui and nationwide, gaped at their phones and TV screens at the magnitude of such devastation.

Although we lived on the other side of the island, the utter grief took hold of my heart. When I thought of each person affected, of the lives that were spared and the lives that weren't, of the utter fear and utter agony and utter loss, my heart couldn't take it.

I didn't personally wrestle with the why, but rather the how. *How can we get through this? How do we grieve as a community? How do we help? How do we come alongside people who have lost everything?* And then there was the survivor's guilt. We were the first to evacuate, and yet our home and family were okay. *Why us and not them?*

A month later, as I felt myself unraveling, and spiraling, and like the whole world was just too heavy, I called Tammy, who can hold the pain with me when I feel like I am sinking in it.

She didn't offer solutions; she didn't offer reasons—she just grieved alongside me.

"Of course you are grieving."

And she offered hope, asking the Lord how I could love in my home in Maui with my community, and in my home with my kids. This was not the time to be supermom, she said. This was not the time to start things up or even to hold anything together. This was the time to slow. To be gentle with myself. To sit and paint my nails with my daughters. To cuddle and watch movies with my kids. To sit outside in the sun and read. To let myself slow as we waited to see how we could serve.

I texted my professor Gerry, grappling with the pain. How do you even begin to understand a natural disaster? He told me, "Alyssa, the only verse in the Bible that is specific to disaster other than ones that are about judgment is Psalm 46:1." I immediately opened my Bible to it:

God is our refuge and strength,
a very present help in trouble.

I couldn't help but smile. It was like salve to my heart. Of course.

When we suffer, it's natural to want to know the why. We grasp for anything that will explain it or give us reasoning for trying to stop something from ever happening again.

But the truth is, even if there was a why, even if we knew the why, that doesn't heal the pain. It doesn't stop the heartache. It doesn't change the outcome.

Think about it. Nowhere in the Bible does it tell us why natural disasters happen. But the one verse we can go to tells us *who* God is in the disaster.

He is strong. He is safe. He is *very present*. And He is our help.

What happened is unexplainable. Sure, the county could have taken more precautions and the power lines could have been more up-to-date, but at the end of the day, you can't stop the hurricane winds from coming. It was completely unimaginable and uncontrollable. We live in a fallen world where natural disasters wreak havoc. And what does God say about it?

He is a very present help in trouble. He comes close.

He is with us in the pain and the agony.

And He aids us in wading through the broken pieces, the heartache, the utter devastation.

Although the expanse of this grief is more communal and specific to our area, I know you can relate to grief. We've all experienced heartache in one way or another, and we will experience more in the future. And we cannot compare our grief with another's. We will always think someone has it harder or worse, but the reality is that no matter what has happened to others, when loss comes knocking at your door, it is devastating.

When you feel like the wind gets knocked out of you.

When sorrow from the news feels unbearable.

When you lose someone, or something, and it seems to sucker punch you in the gut. Over and over again.

The American Psychological Association defines grief in this way: "Grief is the anguish experienced after significant loss, usually the death of a beloved person. Grief often includes physiological distress, separation anxiety, confusion, yearning, obsessive dwelling on the past, and apprehension of the future."[1]

Although we often think of grief as related to the death of a loved one, we can experience grief all throughout life with any loss.

A loss of a relationship.

A loss of health.

A loss of community.

A loss of a home.

A loss of what once was and now isn't.

Our normal is no longer normal. We have to learn to live a new normal, and often that is painful, long, and disorientating. We can experience grief, whether it came on totally out of our control, or we chose it—we chose to move, we chose to set boundaries and end a relationship, we chose to take a new job.

"The greater are our affections the greater are our afflictions," says Bishop J. C. Ryle, "and the more we love the more we have to weep."[2]

The deeper we love a person, the more we hold on to that dream or fully invest in that community or friendship, the deeper our pain may be. The closer that person is to us, the closer the pain hits.

The more that we love someone or something, the more we are invested and rooted and poured into them, or the more we are connected to them like a family member, the more we weep at the loss of it. Sometimes we weep because it was so good and it's no longer, and sometimes we weep because we long for it to change and it hasn't, or it was never what we hoped it would be and now we will never have the chance to see it become what we hoped. Sometimes it is the gift that is ripped away, and sometimes it's the hope and longing that never came to be and now need to be reconciled.

Whatever the grief is, it is an ending. And an ending that we never wanted to happen. How do we continue on with a story that is not what we would have written? And not just in survival mode, but with renewed strength and grace and hope? Is that possible?

I was lying on my back, looking up at the dark brown tongue-and-groove ceiling. To my right was a big moose head. The sun was peeking into the windows from the sunny fall day outside, and as I stretched, worship music was playing in the background. I was in the meeting room at the farm in Vermont, lying on a cream towel that was substituting as my yoga mat.

I crossed my left arm over my chest, and I bent my left knee over my right, and in this position, turned toward the window, I just began to weep. I was surprised by my tears, realizing how long I had held them in. The tears came hot and sudden, and lasted for a long time. I breathed in and admitted to myself how hurt I still was over my friendship losses that year. It had been five months, and although the shock and anger had totally dissipated, the wounds were still open and sensitive. I lay there, letting my heart break. Letting myself feel the agony. Surrendering the dreams I had, the ideals, the hopes that had not come to fruition. And in that space, where I could slow and be, breathe, and take a break from the busy of the day, the needs of others, the constant to-do, I let myself pour out my tears and my aching heart. I put my hand over my chest, as if to hold it together. And I exhaled my pain to God. Finally, I was able to sit with God in my pain, in a posture of gentleness. There was no anger anymore; there were no *should*s or *why*s or *how*s. Rather, I felt like I could come to God as a daughter, broken and longing for His comfort, being met with His father's heart of compassion and mercy.

Grief comes in stages and hits us when we least expect it. It is never linear. Grief cannot be rushed through or ignored, but rather it must be accepted. We cannot manage grief; we can only befriend it. If we do not accept and work through grief, but just stuff it down, it will become anger, which then turns to depression. Sometimes it takes a while to get there. To be willing to accept it, to be willing to look at it. It takes courage to bring it up out of the pit into the light. And that's okay. As long as we actually bring it up. Maybe it's in stages; maybe it's in little steps.

Grief held in the hands of the Father, however, is right where it needs to be. When you bring your grief to Jesus and constantly meet with Him there, letting Him hold your pain, letting Him heal your wounds, moving through your grief with His presence, He will build courage, confidence, joy, and strength in you. A man or woman who has met with God in the fires of life, in the darkest of times, is the one who shines the brightest light. They are like pearls, soft, gentle, and deeply empathetic and incredibly strong. They are not afraid to sit with you in your pain. They do not rush you through it; they do not give you a five-step plan to overcome it; rather, they walk at the pace of Jesus, while holding your heart and your pain and showering you with grace. These people shatter shame. And they reflect the Father's heart, the one full of compassion and grace and kindness. Their formation did not come through ease, or a quick tune-up, or by managing. Rather, their formation came through getting away in the secret place with the Father, lamenting their way through the pain, and doing deep work with wise counselors. And they will be the first to say that the grief never goes away, but it gets easier to live with.

Saint Francis of Assisi said, "All the darkness in the world cannot extinguish the light of a single candle." [3]

We do not need to fear the darkness, the night that is here or will come one day, because, as David says in Psalm 139, "even the darkness is not dark to you [God]" (v. 12). In the hands of the Father, even our darkest of days, or seasons, will not put out the light of the Spirit of God in us, because His light will shine even in the darkest of nights.

So often we run from the pain and suffering of the world because we don't want a broken heart. We don't want to be in pain.

We will face griefs.

And God's love goes there too.

When I have faced pain, in the moments where I can hardly catch my breath because the pain is almost unbearable, I have felt the presence of God the most intimately. Jesus always comes close. He always enters the pain with us. We fear pain so often because we fear that we will be alone in it. However, the opposite is true. Jesus, who is acquainted with our griefs, steps closer. He's not afraid to enter the dark. He's not afraid to get messy. He holds us close.

He was a man of sorrow. If anyone knows our pain, our suffering, our griefs, it's Jesus. No pain is beyond His loving touch.

He was despised and rejected by men,
a man of sorrows and acquainted with grief. (Isaiah 53:3a)

Jesus is Savior, but before He saved, He suffered. He is the Suffering Servant. He is the Man of Grief. He knows it all so well. The utter agony of loss, of rejection, of pain. He is a mighty warrior and the King and the One who has the victory. He defeated death and sin! However, He didn't get to the right hand of God with five easy steps. No. He sits on the throne now because He walked through the darkness then. He had to suffer before He rose. And He did it willingly. He knew what He was signing up for. He took it on, not without a deep wrestle with the Father asking for another way, because of love. There is no pain that Jesus has not experienced or walked through before. He is the Ultimate Empathizer.

My beautiful and passionate friend Cari has this motto: "Come into the unexpected joy of being desperately dependent on God."

Grief does just that. It strips away all illusions, all pretenses, all ideals and causes us to be desperately dependent on God. But the beauty in that is that when we are desperately dependent, we are stronger than ever before. It's the upside-down kingdom. Dependency is strength. And dependency leads to deep joy that cannot come by our doing, but rather our receiving.

Mary, the mother of Jesus, was well acquainted with grief. Luke starts off his gospel telling us about a young teenager, engaged to be married, who is chosen to bear the Son of God. She will have the Holy Spirit come over her and will conceive Jesus.

The angel tells her, "And behold, you will conceive in your womb and bear a son, and you shall call his name Jesus. He will be great and will be called the Son of the Most High. And the Lord God will give to him the throne of his father David, and he will reign over the house of Jacob forever, and of his kingdom there will be no end" (Luke 1:31–33).

Mary sings a song—which was more of a warrior's victory song—of the goodness of God! She receives what the angel tells her, saying, "Behold, I am the servant of the Lord; let it be to me according to your word" (1:38). What a beautiful surrender. A beautiful trust. A beautiful acceptance. She knows how this will look to others. A nonmarried woman pregnant during that time was not acceptable. And yet she trusts God and His plan.

After Jesus is born, she and Joseph take the child to the temple to present Him to the Lord as the firstborn male of the family, and Simeon, the priest at the time, overjoyed at seeing the Messiah, the One promised to Israel, prophesies over Jesus, that He is the One to bring salvation and to be a light to the Gentiles. And then he prophesies to Mary and Joseph and says this to Mary: "Behold, this child is appointed for the fall and rising of many in Israel, and for a sign that is opposed (and a sword will pierce through your own soul also), so that thoughts from many hearts may be revealed" (2:34–35).

Does Mary know that Jesus must suffer before He brings salvation? Does she know this is the way of the Messiah? She knows from Simeon that a sword will pierce her heart; it will be a painful road. But I'm not so sure she had any idea what that sword would be.

And then years later, she is there, front-row seat, watching Jesus hang on that cross. Her Son. Her Savior. Her Rabbi and Messiah. The agony of a death of dreams, of *This isn't what I expected; this is not how the story was supposed to end!* Not to mention the deep despair of losing a child. Oh, how her mother's heart must have cried out.

But then, we fast-forward to the beginning of Acts after Jesus has indeed resurrected and has ascended into heaven and is at the right hand of God, a kingdom inaugurated by Jesus on His throne, and yet the war is not over yet. The disciples are waiting for the Holy Spirit to come upon them as Jesus promised, devoting themselves to prayer, and do you know who is in that room praying with everyone? Mary (1:14).

Mary who conceived the Messiah, raised Him as her Son, was present at His first miracle, followed Him on earth, witnessed His death up close. She is now in the room, praying alongside all of the other disciples—men and women—and she is among the first to receive the Holy Spirit.

It wasn't the story she would have chosen. I highly doubt it was the story she expected. But she witnessed the resurrection and received the Holy Spirit and was among the first of the believers of the church. She conceived the Messiah and received the Holy Spirit. She laid herself open to receive all of God, however the story played out.

I would imagine she was like the rest of the Jews at the time who thought the Messiah would come and defeat the Roman Empire and sit on His rightful throne. They wanted to see justice served here and now, the King exalted here and now, and the war ended here and now.

Sometimes, God moves and works in ways that leave us in complete awe. He raised Lazarus from the dead! He answered your prayer and healed your dad from cancer. He gave you a baby after years of infertility. But oftentimes, we don't get the ending we hope for. Our husband is still sick and suffering. We miscarried. The person we had spent hours counseling turns back to their destructive ways and we never hear from them again. Suicide, death, a wayward child, divorce, a lonely marriage. It feels like the world could swallow us whole sometimes with the weight of the pain and agony.

We know God is with us. But how do we move from point A to point B? How do we move through suffering and actually be transformed in our grief, instead of deformed?

"Lament is where we live, the land between the pain of this earth and the promises of our God," says author and speaker Ann Voskamp.[4]

We must learn to be people of lament. We must learn to passionately grieve and allow ourselves to have sorrow. We are emotional people. We feel. But so often, we fear the feelings that come with pain. The anger. The doubt. The sadness. And our busy lives don't afford us the time to let us feel those things. So we let them simmer, and bubble, until we boil over.

Lament is such a foreign concept in our modern times, but it's a concept that was talked about often in the Jewish ancient culture. At least half of the psalms are laments. Laments are songs and poems where the authors cry out to God in their deep pain and despair. Often, they don't have a resolution. There is no neat bow or happy ending. The Psalms are some of my favorite passages of Scripture, but for years I would skip over these songs of lament. I wanted the happy songs, the rejoicing psalms. But I was missing out on a whole part of God's heart, of connecting my heart to His.

My friend Elizabeth Mosser, who has walked through great suffering, described grief and lament at one of her talks for Intentional Motherhood in this way: Grief is the feeling of deep sorrow that comes out in different ways. It may be in anger, exhaustion, pain in your body, or crying. Lament is what we do with that grief. It's a passionate expression of our grief to God. It's unfiltered, raw, and more healing than we know.

We do not know how to lament. And so, we get stuck. We push grief down, push it aside, try to fix it all. Sometimes we may express our grief to our friends or in our heads, but we stay stuck in our grief and become bitter, hopeless, or cynical because we are not passionately expressing our grief to God. Grief was not meant to stay in our bodies. To stay rattling up in our heads. Grief is meant to, and welcome to, be brought to the Father, in all its forms. Anger, sadness, exhaustion. Lament is our way of healing. It is the only way to move through the grief and to find hope on the other side.

As Elizabeth says, "When we open ourselves up to sorrow, we open ourselves up to deeper joy."

God is not surprised by our grief, nor is He burdened by it. Rather, He is longing to hold us in it. Although lament is not a formula, it is a tool that we must use in order to move through grief.

Read any of the lament psalms, and you will see that the authors were gut honest with God. They held nothing back. They lamented individually and communally. And if you study the lament psalms, you can start to see a structure to a lot of them. Some end with a happy bow of praising God, but others do not—they simply are expressed feelings that are being poured out. Sometimes our lament will lead us to wait, and hope will appear; other times it may just be us pouring out our raw and honest hearts before God and having Him sit there with us in it. It's okay to not have it end happy. To sit in the tension. To sit with the pain and not have the joy yet.

A lot of laments in the Psalms consist of the following:

An address—cry it out to God.

Lament—here's my pain, my cry.

A confession of trust—you know God is trustworthy, even if you don't feel it.

A petition—ask God to do something.

Waiting—we often miss this because it's subtle in the psalms. It's hard to track time in writing because we read ahead. But this is key to lament. It takes time.

A transformation—good will come, hope will come, joy will come. Eventually. In God, all things work together for good for those who love Him. Even if the thing is not good, God will work it out for *your* good. He is all about making beauty out of ashes.

For instance, if we look at Psalm 27:7–14, we'll see these come into play. I want to use *The Message* here just to show you how gut honest we can be with God:

David addresses the Lord: "Listen, GOD, I'm calling at the top of my lungs."

He then laments: "You've always been right there for me; don't turn your back on me now. Don't throw me out, don't abandon me."

Then he confesses his trust: "My father and mother walked out and left me, but GOD took me in."

He asks the Lord, "Point me down your highway, GOD; direct me along a well-lighted street; show my enemies whose side you're on. Don't throw me to the dogs."

And then at the end, we're not sure how long he waits with God there in that space, but finally he says, "I'm sure now I'll see God's goodness in the exuberant earth." He cries out in pain, while also crying out in hope. But that hope came through the lament. Hope came through the tears.

He takes it even one step further and talks to others: "Stay with GOD! Take heart. Don't quit. I'll say it again: Stay with GOD."

The beauty of this psalm is that it shows us how prayer is not something we tiptoe into with timidity, but it is God inviting us into His presence; it's a divine invitation. And as one commentator said once, "Prayer is impregnated with confidence."[5]

Psalm 27:5 in the ESV says, "For he will hide me in his shelter in the day of trouble; he will conceal me under the cover of his tent; he will lift me high upon a rock."

David, although lamenting and begging God to not hide from him, also confidently knows that he is hidden with God even in the midst of his enemies.

Eugene Peterson says this about honest prayers: "We must pray who we actually are, not who we think we should be...In prayer, all is not sweetness and light. The way of prayer is not to cover our unlovely emotions so that they will appear respectable, it's to expose them so that they can be enlisted in the work of the kingdom."[6]

Grief probably won't come out so cleanly and orderly as it

does in this psalm. We must know that before these words were penned, David agonized and grieved; and he probably agonized and grieved even as he wrote. I wouldn't be surprised if many of his scrolls were covered with tears. But when we lament, and when we go to God in our lament, after time, we can rest assured that hope will come. Transformation will come. Our hearts will begin to beat again. They will begin to hope again. We will be able to tell others eventually of the goodness of God. To utter our confidences once again. But we have to go to God. Let it all out. Let our hearts break before Him, where His heart breaks for us and holds us and weeps with us, to then come out on the other side with assurance of God's deep care and love.

The problem comes when we go to something other than God to take the pain of grief away. Of course, healing comes in different ways. Sometimes grief can lead us to create beauty. After I had miscarried, learning to oil paint became such a healing tool in my life. To learn to create beauty in the midst of birthing death. Girls' nights spent eating frozen gummy worms and watching reruns of *Friends* after devastating breakups is fun and comforting. However, no one meets us in our times of utter pain as Jesus does. No one can hold our pain as Jesus does, and no one can renew us with hope as the Savior does.

But that means we must come to Jesus, again and again, crying out to Him, telling Him our sorrow, our despair, our questions. We must notice the pain in our bodies and present it to Jesus.

God, my heart feels broken. My lungs are having a hard time breathing. I feel hollow inside. I feel angry. I feel in shock.

It's messy and may feel chaotic and out of our control. We may yell, we may wail, we may punch a pillow or lie in our bed for hours in the fetal position. It may take days, months, years longer than we anticipated. But it's all about coming back to Him. Crying to Him. And waiting to see how He meets us.

He wants to hold your pain. He wants to grieve with you.

God doesn't just care for you, but He holds all your tears. His heart breaks when your heart breaks. As Ann Voskamp says in *The Broken Way,* "You never cry alone."[7]

Saint Ephraim says, "Until you have cried, you don't know God."[8]

I was on a Zoom call with a group of women I get to lead and gather, and my professor Gerry was our guest for the day. He has walked with countless people through so much pain and suffering, and he himself has experienced much pain as he has done so. I had asked him to share with us how to continue to stay steadfast in life, even when it's hard.

As we entered into the Q-and-R time, my friend who has experienced suffering in her home asked Gerry with weary eyes, "How do we not lose heart?"

Gerry immediately responded, "Sometimes you will lose heart."

He paused. And then said, "But in that losing heart, you don't lose God."

My paradigm of Christianity shifted that day. I thought as people of God we weren't supposed to lose heart. I thought we were to always stay hopeful.

Second Corinthians 4:16–18 says,

So we do not lose heart. Though our outer self is wasting away, our inner self is being renewed day by day. For this light momentary affliction is preparing for us an eternal weight of glory beyond all comparison, as we look not to the things that are seen but to the things that are unseen. For the things that are seen are transient, but the things that are unseen are eternal.

Yes, in this passage Paul is explaining how we do not lose heart because of the glory that is being prepared for us. But here's the thing: we have to lose our heart in God's before we don't lose heart. When we think that we need to manage our grief, it manages us, and we don't give ourselves the chance to grieve in the hands of the Man of Sorrows. We have to be honest with God about how we have lost heart in order to not lose heart. It's the in-between. We lose heart, practice lament, so we can win back our heart. And this may have long stretches between each comma, and may be a needed circling rather than step by step to fruition.

It's only when we cry out to God with the utter pain of our brokenness that we experience His "withness" and take heart because we are, in fact, never alone. The thing that we want most in life—unconditional love—is actually with us always. Grace is our grounding. Jesus knows our pain intimately, and instead of giving us a formula or a plan, He gives us Himself. His presence. And it's in His presence that we can get a glimpse into the unseen, like Paul, and see that these griefs today that feel oh so weighty are, in fact, light compared to the weight of the glory that we will experience. But we have to look to the unseen; we have to look to Jesus.

In *The Great Divorce*, C. S. Lewis describes what heaven will be like by explaining the weight of glory.[9] He gives a picture of a bus of dead people arriving at purgatory, which he calls the gray town. They soon realize that they are ghostlike, but everything around them is full of weight and glory. Lewis describes the gray town and how the ghostlike people who did not follow Jesus and were not transformed into their glorious selves keep cutting their feet on the grass because the grass is so dense and sharp, and they are so thin and airy. This is the glory that awaits us. A world that is so magnificent, so full of God, that everything is weighty and dense. So much more real and glorious than anything we could imagine. The griefs that we carry on earth will seem light when we experience His glory one day. We look forward to the promise in Revelation that says, "He will wipe away every tear from their eyes, and death shall be no more, neither shall there be mourning, nor crying, nor pain anymore, for the former things have passed away" (Rev. 21:14 ESV).

As we wait for that day, God wades through the heavy griefs with us, ministering to our weary hearts and causing our hearts to feel lighter and lighter as we continue to look to Him and cry out to Him.

We are jars of clay that get broken and cracked and chipped, but we hold the treasure of Jesus in us. Christ in us. The hope of glory. It's in this very jar of clay that He shines forth.

Psalm 118:14 says, "The LORD is my strength and my song."

Exhaustion can come from all the things we try to accomplish, but it also can come from all that we try to manage internally. We can feel completely undone by such inner pain. We sometimes believe the lie that a Christian woman is to not be emotional, or at least not have ugly emotions. We need to be happy all the time, thankful for the life God has given us; we need to not doubt, to not question, to certainly not be angry. But we are not meant to hold all of that pain in our bodies on our own. We are meant to be His vessels, to be full of the Holy Spirit, to let Him flow in and through us. But we cannot flow with grace and love if we have dammed up our emotions and thoughts. God did not say we can't be angry. He said do not sin in your anger. He welcomes, invites, and insists that we lament our pain and sorrow to Him, to the One who grieves alongside us and holds us and knows what it is to grieve.

God grieves throughout the Bible, starting in the beginning in Genesis 6:6: "And the LORD regretted that he had made man on the earth, and it grieved him to his heart" because man was so sinful. God the Father agonized at Jesus' death on the cross. Jesus agonized at His own death on the cross. Jesus wept when Lazarus died. He didn't just shed a tear—no, he wept. David, who learned to lament, was a man after God's own heart. Jeremiah was a weeping prophet.

Jesus welcomes your tears. He welcomes your grief.

God promises to hold your tears (Ps. 56:8). The Holy Spirit is called our comforter (John 14:26).

God longs to hold you close to His heart. To wipe away your tears. To walk with you in the pain and suffering, walking toward wholeness and healing and hope.

We grieve, but we do not grieve as those who are without hope (1 Thess. 4:13).

But hope does not come automatically. We cannot command or demand it. We must go with God, letting our hearts spill out to Him, and there, we will find hope. We will find God. In the midst of our pain and sorrow.

Go to God in your grief.

Spiritual Practice

Have you ever lamented before? Do you create space for those who are grieving to lament with you? Or do you try to fix things, find the answer, find the way to reason, and move on?

Lamenting is not for lament's sake. It is for the sake of finding hope, but in order to do so, you must walk through grief.

Is your heart breaking over something today? What are you grieving? Get away by yourself. Cry, yell, question, sit until the emotions come. Don't give yourself a timeframe or a set of goals. No judgment here. Let yourself cry your tears to God and wait for His presence to be near to you.

If this is too difficult, or after you've done this alone, ask a friend or mentor to lament with you. This is an exercise in vulnerability and letting community walk with you. It is a gift to both you and them.

PART IV

FULLNESS OF HEART

We have seen how we can neglect our hearts by not "going there," and how we can try to gain strength of heart by looking to others and things to control so we can be proven worthy, and then how we can, quite frankly, lose heart because life is hard. Disappointments, broken dreams, and grief and sorrow can come like a thief in the night, leaving us gasping for breath and living in a fog.

In all of these, we have learned that God has a better way. He cares about our hearts. They matter to Him and He longs to be united to us, to be one, to be connected. The sweet surprise and grace are that it's in these very things—in the trying to stuff our feelings down, in our attempts at performance, and in the despair—that He invites us to come to Him. To bring Him our exhausted, weary, and exasperated selves. To come to Him just as we are, completely undone, in the unwanted moments, with our deepest of emotions, and be refreshed, unburdened by His presence. By the light of His face.

This next section is a picture of who we become as we come to Him. It is a description of living with fullness of heart. God longs to abide in us, to let His Spirit flow freely and abundantly in and through us, and as we walk with Him, as we look to Him, obeying Him and opening up our hearts to Him, we will be transformed to be more and more like Jesus. Not by our control, but rather by our rest. The greatest gift we can give others is our transformed self, not managing the outcomes for them. So let's take a look at how we can be transformed into His image—as people of love, peace, and joy, regardless of our circumstances and the outcomes of life.

11

LOVE EMBODIED

At the center of care for the heart is the love of God. This must be the joyful aim of our life.   —DALLAS WILLARD

As we walk with God, and continue to come to Him, again and again, and continue to unburden ourselves by releasing our heaviness to Him and receiving what He wants to give us—soul rest and a soul that is fully alive—we start to shed our false selves and become our true selves. Our truest self is not what the world teaches us—that to be an authentic human, we have to live out of what we *feel*, not submitting to any authority or truth. Rather, our true self is what God lays out for us. It's when we, believers with regenerate hearts, live out of our deepest desires—to connect our hearts to God and to let love flow in and out of us.

We all long for this. This is what we really want.

The temptation is to control the outcomes of our lives, to manage it all so that it goes well for us and those around us. To try to control our lives so we can hold everything together. But as we've seen, that only leads to us feeling exhausted and weary, and in fact, it unravels us. Control is an illusion. It's like a mirage in the desert that we keep chasing after, but it only leaves us thirsty and depleted.

However, when we walk with God, following His ways, learning to release expectations, ideals, and control, and receiving His presence and all that flows out of His character—love, compassion, grace, mercy, tenderness, gentleness—we start to become more and more like Him.

We start to reflect Him.

Biblical scholar G. K. Beale says, "What you revere, you resemble, either for ruin or for restoration."[1]

We revere success and ease and happiness, running from pain and loss in our lives, and we become fragmented and depleted.

But when we revere God, longing to be with Him and partner with Him in whatever He is doing, and seeing that as the highest aim, the greatest gift, we become people who are free, radiant, and glorious because we start to reflect the One whom we adore. We're able to let go of the outcomes, to accept our realities because God is there with us in them. His "withness" is the strength our hearts really desire. And we start to run free. Light.

As we sit with Jesus, receiving His love that He has for us, we start to become people of love, letting His love flow through us to love those around us.

Love can be a tricky word sometimes because it's so overused. We use it with everything. I love my kids, and I love special fizzy drinks. I love my friends, and I love pickleball.

So what does it really mean when we say we want to become people of love? And that God loves us?

It means that we don't just know He loves us in our heads, but we experience His love and receive it fully. It means that we don't just say we love others, but we actually embody love and have others experience it in our presence.

I love the sun. And ironically, I grew up in Seattle where the sun only comes out three months of the year. But let me tell ya, for those three months you better believe I was outside for every single moment of sunshine to bask in its warmth. Seattle in the summer truly is one of the most beautiful places in the world. In high school, as soon as class was out at the end of the day, I would rush home, throw on my bathing suit, and lie out on my trampoline in our backyard until dusk (back in the day when my goal in life was to get a tan—I did it like it was my part-time job). It was glorious. I lived for those days.

We now live in a place that is sunny all year long. (Proof that God does miracles today! Won't He do it!) I fell in love with Hawaii when I moved here after college to work as an intern at our church. The moment I got off the plane and was welcomed with a lei full of fragrant plumerias, palm trees swaying, and the sun shining down on my pale face, I knew I wanted to live here for the rest of my life.

God just had to get Jeff on board once we were married! And He did. After three years of praying that we could move back to Hawaii, Jeff's heart changed overnight, and we moved in a matter of a few months.

Even to this day I can't wait to get out on our front porch with a cup of hot coffee in my hand and look up at the sun. I bask in it. I can't help but smile under its weight and light.

On mornings when the sun isn't coming out, I use my red-light therapy. I'll lie in bed and close my eyes and let that bad boy do its magical work on my skin for twelve minutes. (Well, I think it's doing magical work. It makes me happy like the sun and is supposed to help with wrinkles and aging.) I sit there and pray and think about the Lord, and honestly, it's my favorite twelve minutes in my day.

Now, this analogy might be a bit cheesy, but go with me here for a minute. The sun is a lot like God's love. It's warm, inviting, and healing. We grow up hearing how God loves us, and we know it to be true in our heads, but often we don't believe it with our hearts. We don't know how it can penetrate our lives in our moments of shame, of guilt, of despair and hopelessness and just flat-out chaos and burden. We don't live loved. And so we live exhausted.

The problem is that we don't bask in His love. We take it as a truth and then go about our days. However, what good is head knowledge if it doesn't transform us? We must learn to soak in His love, to encounter His love and experience it. Just like the sun gives off vitamin D and makes us happy, as well as gives us a nice glowing tan (sorry to those who burn; maybe take the sun and exchange it for an infrared sauna that heals your body inside and out), so spending time with Jesus lets His warm glow shine on and in and through us. But just like we need vitamin D every day, and our tans can fade, so we need to be with Jesus daily as well. To nourish ourselves with His presence, to soak ourselves in His Word, to be with His people.

David Benner says in *Surrender to Love*, "It is not the fact of being loved unconditionally that is life changing. It is the *risky experience of allowing* myself to be loved unconditionally"[2] (italics mine).

It's one thing to know in our heads that God loves us, but it's a totally different thing to experience His love. But in order to experience it, we have to let ourselves be loved.

Jeff surprised me with a trip to Nevis this past year for our tenth wedding anniversary. It was the end of hurricane season, so no one was really on the island; it felt like we had it to ourselves. One morning I threw on my swimsuit and walked the beach by myself. I have never seen water like the Caribbean. I mean, Hawaii water is gorgeous, but the Caribbean is glass. You can see straight down to the bottom of the ocean. There are no waves—it's just crystal-clear aqua water that is warm and calm. As I started to walk, I talked to Jesus. I was pouring out my heart to Him, telling Him how grateful I was for this trip, for this rare time with just Jeff, for how He (Jesus) was my truest Friend and the true Lover of my soul. He had done such a work in me that fall. Through my healing of the wounds I carried, through my aloneness that I thought would be lonely but actually turned out to be a great gift because I got to experience His presence, He showered me with His love. In all the little ways He does. Through the sunlight gleaming through the fall trees, or the way the squirrels ran up the trunks and peeked over at me with acorns in their little paws. I would talk to Him every day, pouring it all out, asking Him questions, crying out my hurt, telling Him my worries, and He would meet me there. He would give me a truth, remind me of His care, help me to forgive.

And here I was, doing the same thing, but now on a beach instead of a forest path. I was so overwhelmed by His faithful love. As I was talking to Him, I kept my gaze on the water's edge, looking for seashells, one of my favorite pastimes. I looked down in the water, and there was part of a conch shell—the kind that looks like a horn, that the Hawaiians blow when the sun goes down into the ocean every evening, and the kind that you see watercolor paintings of. They're gorgeous, and this Caribbean beach was covered in them. But this particular one was different. I picked it up, and lo and behold, it was in the shape of a ring! It had been chiseled down by the waves over and over until it literally had a hole to put your finger through, and it looked like a rose. I grabbed it, slid it onto my finger, and it fit perfectly. A ring, just for me.

It was as though the Lord was whispering to my tender heart, "Alyssa, you are mine. I love you. I love being yours. I love that you are mine. Forever."

It was a moment of surprise, but isn't that the way of Jesus? To meet us right where we're at. To know our hearts so intimately. To bring us to a place of basking in His love.

We can experience His love every day. It looks different every day. But God loves to come where He's wanted. He longs to meet us. Yes, He meets us at church, or in a Bible study, or on a retreat. But He also will meet us in the kitchen, in the laundry room, in the car, or at night while we lie in our beds. Space and time are so needed to let our heads get connected with our hearts, and to let our hearts get connected to Him—and we need to pursue that space. But He also understands our limits and responsibilities and can come meet us wherever, as long as we're asking. It's as we come, answering the call of His invitation, that He meets us.

Sometimes His love comes in quiet whispers, other times like loud wind. Sometimes it's a small thought or truth; sometimes it's a long conversation. Sometimes it's through someone else— through a hug, their care, their listening ear or prayer. Other times it's as we sit and rest and talk to Him, or when we go out in nature and bask in the beauty He created.

One of my favorite ways I experience God's love is to sit and picture myself in my safe place. Often, it's not even a real place, but it's a place I picture in my mind that feels peaceful. Sometimes I picture myself in our yard during golden hour, on this bench where butterflies are flying around me. Other times I picture myself next to a window above the lake, looking out as the sun hits the waves like a thousand diamonds. I go there in my mind, and I picture Jesus sitting down with me. He sits close. I try to think of what it feels like to be in His presence. It's always warm, always inviting. Always hopeful. And then I try to look at His face. In His eyes. Eyes that are always soft, always open, always loving. They are never scornful or shaming. They invite. And it's here, in this space, that I talk to God. I tell Him my heart. My fears, my doubts, my feelings. I listen for what He wants me to know, what truth He wants to give me. Sometimes the Spirit convicts, and I repent, not out of shame, but always out of His kindness. Sometimes He comforts and consoles. Sometimes He smiles and laughs, and sometimes He speaks direction and guidance. And other times, we just sit together in my mind and enjoy each other's company. Whatever happens here, it always aligns with Scripture; it is rooted in what God says about Himself.

His love is all around us. But we have to be awake to it. Awake to Him. Awake to our own hearts.

We have to seek Him to find Him. It starts with curiosity. It begins with a posture of humility, of need.

My friend Emily quoted her mentor to me once, saying, "Christian maturity is not about how much we know about God, but it's about how much we are willing to receive from God."

I believe that a life lived with Jesus is a life full of releasing (all that is not of Him, that is not ours to carry), receiving (all His love and goodness and hope), and then giving (giving all that we have received from God away to others; His kingdom is a generous kingdom). Release, receive, give.

The Christian life is not about what we can do for God, but rather, what we receive from God, and then learning to live in complete abandonment and confidence in Him, giving Him away to others.

His love is poured out into our hearts day by day through the Spirit, the One who is compared to living water (John 7:38). Always flowing, running freely, never ending.

However, there are things that block His love from flowing through us. For instance, bitterness, jealousy, selfish ambition, and unforgiveness can all make us stuck and make us become people who withhold love and don't live loved. We will get hurt, we will be sinned against, we will be tempted to want what someone else has, or to try to earn love or acceptance. But we have a choice to forgive in Jesus' name, by His Spirit, or to let the unforgiveness make its home in our hearts and grow bitter and hard. We have the choice to be envious of what someone else has, or to bless them and give thanks for what God has given to us. We have a choice to trust in our own efforts and will, or to walk with God, and entrust our longings to Him and rest in His ability to bring about the outcome.

This fall I found myself very hurt and struggling to not give up hope in one of my relationships. I loved this person to my core, and yet thoughts of bitterness and hurt just kept swirling in my head and settling in my heart. One morning, as I cuddled on the couch and watched the sunrise from the living room, I opened up *Soul Keeping* by John Ortberg[3] and found myself reading his chapter on blessing and cursing.

In it he said two things that profoundly changed my perspective.

1. He said that there is no neutral thought or word. Whatever you say, or think, is either blessing someone or cursing someone.
2. He quoted Dallas Willard, who said that when you find yourself becoming jealous of someone or starting to compare or compete with them or cursing them, ask the Lord to bless that person *more than* you, to give them *more* success than you, to show them *more* favor than you.

Immediate tears stung my eyes. In an instant I was convicted and cut to the heart, and also given fresh life.

How many times had I cursed this person in my head? Thinking of all that could change, of all that wasn't happening, of all that they weren't? How many times had I tried to compete with and prove myself to or at least be equal with this person? On their same playing field.

It was as if I had been throwing fuel on the fire. And it was only wreaking havoc on my heart. Love was blocked. I was withholding it.

Later that week I went for a long walk, planning on getting a good workout in. As I started to walk, my heart was heavy with the pain of this relationship. With each step, the tears came. Hot and fervent. I was thankful to be wearing sunglasses to hide behind!

As I veered up the path, there was this swinging bench on the side, and I felt the Lord tell me to sit and release. To let it all out. To cry it all out.

And I did. I sat there, swinging and weeping. But I felt the Lord's presence so close. He was with me in the sadness, in the heartache, in the pain. I could cry all my tears out to Him. And as I cried, and repented of my cursing, I started to see the blessing. I started to see all that was good. All that God was doing. All that this person was that was a gift to me. I was able to decipher better what really was hard, what really was needing more healing, and what was good. And the good made me hold on to more hope. God was not done. God was still working even when I couldn't see.

And regardless of what the other person chose or how long change would take, the Lord was faithfully forming me into a woman of love and grace.

As I walked back to the house, the circumstances hadn't changed, but my heart had done a one-eighty. Instead of being full of despair and holding so fast to my hurt, I was able to hold fast to hope and be full of love for this person, for me, and for God.

Blessing is like letting the floodgates open and letting His love flow through us. It allows us to see others with His eyes—with His eyes of compassion and mercy. It allows us to have hearts of gratefulness and joy instead of scarcity and cynicism.

There is no neutrality. It is either blessing or cursing. Which will we choose?

But we cannot muster up love on our own strength. It's only as we sit with the Father, soaking in His love for us, that we can then give love to others, that we can then truly bless them. We can only give away what we possess.

Love is a softness of heart toward others. Love is forgiveness. Love is repentance. Love is patient and faithful and gentle and hopeful.

In order to fully love others, we must receive the full love of Jesus. We can only give what we have. If we want to be known as loving people, we must learn to first sit in God's love and receive His love.

Benner says,

Meet God in a contemplative state—sitting at the feet of Jesus, gazing at his face and listening to his assurance of love for me. It comes from letting God's love wash over me, not simply trying to believe it. It comes from soaking in the scriptural assurances of such love, not simply reading them and trying to remember or believe them. It comes from spending time with God, observing how he looks at me. It comes from watching his watchfulness over me and listening to his protestations of love for me.[4]

And as we sit with Jesus, we have to be honest about any bitterness, unforgiveness, or envy we are storing up in our hearts.

Are you bitter because you thought your life would look a certain way and doesn't, and you feel like it's God's fault? Are you bitter that you don't have what you wanted and feel like God is withholding from you?

Do you hold bitterness toward someone? For how they let you down, how they weren't faithful to their word, for some way they hurt you or sinned against you?

Is there anyone that you are withholding forgiveness from? Anyone that you have a hard heart toward? Anyone you think of with disdain in your heart? Anyone who you are holding so close in their sins against you and not letting them go? No, forgiveness does not mean we never remember it again, but it's choosing to forgive them and building an altar there so when the hurt or thoughts come up again, you can remember how you forgave them there, in that moment. It's a line in the sand.

Is there any sin that you've committed that you need to ask forgiveness for? Any way that you've sinned against someone? Hurt someone, were careless with your words, were hard-hearted toward them? Do you need to make it right?

Is there anyone that you are envious of? Jealous of? Her body, her house, her husband, her family, her career, her finances, her season of life? How quickly envy can come rushing into my thoughts, and yet how slow I can be to recognize it at times. It can be detrimental to a relationship, for who can stand under envy? It is one thing to weep with others who are going through pain; it's another thing to rejoice with those who are rejoicing. It takes such a lack of jealousy, such a heart of true love toward them. Such a heart of trusting in God's utter abundance and goodness to you, not based on circumstances, but based on His relationship that is always freely offered, never withheld.

The thing is, if we are holding any of these things in our hearts with others, it blocks the love of God from flowing into our hearts. We cannot know the love of God, and we cannot draw deeper into intimacy with Him if we are holding on to unforgiveness or envy or bitterness. Sometimes our weariness and exhaustion come because we're so busy replaying in our minds and storing in our bodies the hurt that others have caused us. We spend so much time thinking of our pain, of the words that were said, and the love withheld. Unforgiveness wields a cavern of exhaustion and burden deep in our souls. And even though we try to hold ourselves together, we, in fact, become undone.

But it's in the undone, in the unraveling that God invites us to come to Him and work it out with Him. To confess, to repent, to admit, and to surrender. He wants to give us love and peace and joy in exchange for the bitterness and envy and unforgiveness.

When Moses came down from the mountain, shining with God's glory, his skin literally glowed. Perhaps his skin was hardened. Similar to when we sunbathe all day, and our skin becomes like leather from the sun. It's tougher.

It's in the presence of God, in the presence of light, that our hearts are strengthened, our skin toughened to face the hardships of life, while our hearts remain and become even softer. His presence keeps us vulnerable, but it's not about living in a place of vulnerability and being exposed; rather, it's exposing our vulnerability to the Lord. It's here that He gives us security and toughness, while making our hearts tender.

We must look to Him, spend time face-to-face with the God who loves us far more abundantly than we could ever think or imagine.

Ephesians 3:16–19 states,

That according to the riches of his glory he may grant you to be strengthened with power through his Spirit in your inner being, so that Christ may dwell in your hearts through faith—that you, being rooted and grounded in love, may have strength to comprehend with all the saints what is the breadth and length and height and depth, and to know the love of Christ that surpasses knowledge, that you may be filled with all the fullness of God.

God wants to strengthen us with the power of the Holy Spirit. How does He do that? As we root ourselves in His love. Not only are we strengthened to understand His unfathomable love, but we are also filled with all His fullness as we find ourselves in His love.

So often we neglect our hearts, try to earn our hearts, or lose heart because we fail to see God's love for us. Oh, daughter, you are not what you do. God is not after your performance. He is after your heart. And He longs to be one with you in heart. To draw close, to beckon you to Himself and to be known by you and to know you fully.

You do not need to hold it all together. You just need to hold on to Him.

And as you do, let Him search your heart. Ask Him to show you any way that is not of Him. Remember, it's His kindness that will lead you to repentance, not shame.

My friend Alisa Keeton always tells me, "Try softer, Alyssa." God is not harsh with us, so we need to be soft with ourselves.

Unforgiveness, bitterness, and burden will keep you away from Him and from letting His love freely flow through you.

My two older kids Kinsley and Kannon love the worship song "I Thank God" by Maverick City Music. My favorite line of the song is "Burden and bitter night...you ain't welcome here."

I belt that line every time! Come to Him, letting Him search your heart, and let His love flow in you. Open up the door and kick out the unwanted guests of bitterness and burden. Those are not of Him. They are not welcome here anymore.

In Jesus' name, they can be cast out to make room for His presence to flood your heart, your mind, and your soul, giving you real strength.

Spiritual Practice

If you can, go sit out in the sunshine today. Let it hit your face and soak up its warmth. Thank the Lord that He loves you with such warmth and delight and grace. Put on some "soaking" music. (William Augusto is my favorite. It's instrumental music that causes my heart and mind to slow and truly sit in God's love.)

Ask Jesus these questions:

1. Is there anywhere in your life that you have a hard time receiving His love?
2. Is there anyone in your life that you are cursing and not blessing? What would it look like for you to receive love in that area and to bless that person?

12

PRACTICING PEACE

I bet that one of the reasons you picked up this book is because you are longing for peace. You want your days to go smoothly, your plans to go accordingly, your mind to be steady, and your heart to be whole. You long to not be agitated or irritable or anxious.

And yet life has left you feeling anything but peaceful. It can feel scary, frantic, fragmented. You may walk through your day with a heart that beats too fast, and hands that sweat, and a mind that races. Your breathing gets shortened, and your shoulders get tight.

Or maybe anxiety shows up more in the margins of life, when you are alone in bed at night, or in the car, and you can finally let it all out, and tears come in waves.

This is not how I want my life to go.

This is not how it's supposed to be!

You find yourself utterly wiped out. Coming undone. Falling apart.

You long for peace. You know that God is a God of peace and came to give us peace, and yet it feels like a wistful dream.

How can I have peace, let alone be a person of peace, in this chaotic, crazy, out-of-my-control life?

And so we turn to control or knowledge to try to find peace.

We try to manage people, circumstances, our days in a way that keeps the peace. But in reality, that's just keeping all that's needed to be looked at and discovered at bay. We try to stop the undoing while not realizing we just prolong it and stay stuck.

It's a false peace. And it leaves us feeling anything but peace.

True peace comes when we can face the pain, the unknowns, the uncomfortable and go there with Jesus.

True peace is, in fact, not dependent on our circumstances; instead, it's completely dependent on *whom* we are depending on.

Are you relying on yourself or your circumstances to find peace? Or are you drawing near to the Father and receiving the peace that He has to give you?

Peace is not something you can fabricate; it is, in fact, a gift to receive and steward.

I hate flying. It's ironic because it's a huge part of what Jeff and I do (not to mention we live in the middle of the Pacific Ocean on an island whose closest land mass is two thousand miles away! In my head I'm shouting that sentence as if to implement how truly far we are from everyone!), and yet every time I hop on a plane to go somewhere, my heart starts to beat rapidly, and I have to focus on my breathing. Now, the concept of travel I love. I love exploring the world and meeting people from all over and being part of the global church. I just don't enjoy how I get to those places in the world. Planes feel so vulnerable. So not in my control.

I was flying home from Salt Lake City this last winter break with the kids and my parents—which was our first problem. Flying in the winter, you're always bound for some bad weather. We had a connecting flight in San Diego, where apparently there was a huge storm raging. I thought for sure San Diego would be our best bet—you know, stay south, away from snow and storms! But no, as we neared San Diego, the clouds became dense all around us, and their white became pitch-black. I could not see the ground at all, and all of a sudden, our plane started dropping, then flying up and going side to side. My hands grasped the armrests, and I closed my eyes. I tried not to freak out for my four-year-old Lucy's sake, because she was sitting next to me, looking at the storm, then looking at me. She wasn't worried, so I tried to not look too worried either. The other two kids were totally unaware as they stared at their screens. But I was soaked through with sweat. I held my head down between my legs and just prayed we'd land safely.

Clearly, I am here today to tell you we made it! As soon as we landed, I looked back at my parents with horrified eyes. I told them I was not okay, and my dad, in his ever-easy-going spirit, said, "Oh, Alyssa, if anything did ever happen, we'd die so quickly it'd be okay." Sure, but I just don't want to go out that way!

Now, some of you crazy people love turbulence and think it's like a fun roller-coaster ride. I applaud you and tell you that I am not you. I wish I were! I wish I could see it as an adventure, but instead, I freak out every time because I feel so uneasy, and there's *nothing* I can do about it except grasp for my lavender patches for my wrists and suck on my "no stress" lozenges.

I love peaceful trips, with not a hint of turbulence. The kind where you can just enjoy your ride and read or study or watch your shows. Those are a joy. But when that little bit of wind hits, I duck for cover.

It's similar to my life. I long for unbumpy days. I long for a peaceful inner being and a peaceful outer life. But the reality is a lot of days are bumpy, with unexpected turbulence. God says we can still have peace within and exude peace without. But how?

Matthew 14 tells the popular story of how Jesus met His disciples out on the water. They were in a boat, and He was walking on the water. Can you imagine? He wasn't hydrofoiling, but He was actually walking on the water, defying all gravity. At first the disciples were scared, shouting, "It's a ghost" (v. 26 NIV). It was just before dawn, and they had been sailing all night. I'm sure they were tired and thought their eyes were playing tricks on them, or that it truly was a ghost. No man had walked on water before. What were they to make of it?

Wanting to dismiss all fear, Jesus immediately says, "Take courage! It is I. Don't be afraid" (v. 27 NIV).

It wasn't a ghost. It wasn't a trick of their eyes or a bad spirit. But it was their Lord, their Rabbi, coming to meet them in the most unconventional way. He was defying gravity to come and be with them.

Peter, the ever-bold Peter, says, "Lord, if it's you...tell me to come to you on the water" (v. 28 NIV). My professor says, "Peter is able to sense the miracle zone and asks to enter in."

"Come," Jesus said (v. 29).

And so Peter gets out of the boat and, I'm sure to his shock and awe, starts walking on the water. What was it like? Did it feel like he was floating? Did it feel like he was walking on concrete?

What we do know is that he was walking toward Jesus, but as soon as he saw the wind, he became afraid and began to sink.

The text doesn't say this, but I always assume Peter was looking at Jesus as he was walking. Keeping his eyes on Him completely. Totally locked, like you lock your eyes on a nonmoving object when you're trying to balance in a yoga pose. But as soon as he took his eyes off of Jesus and put his focus on the wind, on the shaking circumstance around him, he became afraid and sank.

Jesus immediately saves him and says, "You of little faith, why did you doubt?" (v. 31).

Now, Jesus doesn't say that condescendingly, nor does He say it in a shaming manner. Rather, I sense His love and compassion and His sorrow: *Why would you doubt Me? Why would you doubt My ability to care for you? Don't you know I am over the wind? I calm the storm.*

John tells us Jesus' words in John 14:26–27 (MSG):

The Friend, the Holy Spirit whom the Father will send at my request, will make everything plain to you. He will remind you of all the things I have told you. I'm leaving you well and whole. That's my parting gift to you. Peace. I don't leave you the way you're used to being left—feeling abandoned, bereft. So don't be upset. Don't be distraught.

Jesus goes on to say in John 16:33, "I've told you all this so that trusting me, you will be unshakable and assured, deeply at peace. In this godless world you will continue to experience difficulties. But take heart! I've conquered the world."

The word *peace* in these verses is the Greek word *eirene*, and it alludes to "the tranquil state of a soul assured of its salvation through Christ, and so fearing nothing from God and content with its earthly lot, of whatsoever sort that is."[1]

God wants to give us peace. He wants to be our firm foundation. But peace does not come from our circumstances, from looking around us at what we can count on or what we think will hold us up. Rather, peace comes from looking to Jesus, our eyes set on Him. Peace comes from the Holy Spirit, our Helper, our Advocate; it comes from our *withness* of God.

So often I think peace comes from not rocking the boat, not saying the hard things, not sharing my true heart, because it could upset someone or upset me. I want to stay calm. I want to stay neutral.

I don't want to face conflict, because I don't want to be exhausted, but in fact, not facing it makes me so much more exhausted. Weary. Fraught with anxiety.

Neutrality is death.

No thought is neutral.

God does not want us to be neutral. He wants us to be alive.

Peace often comes as we go through the hard.

It comes as we do the hard inner work of being honest with ourselves about what we're feeling and why.

It comes as we have the uncomfortable conversation with someone and are honest about our hurts, or lovingly say things that need to be said.

It comes as we set boundaries and are clear about what we need. Clarity is kindness.

It comes as we seek wisdom from God, from mentors, from friends and parents that we trust.

Peace comes from doing all that we can, regardless of how the other person responds. Regardless of whether the outcome turns out the way we hope. It comes regardless of whether there's closure. It comes by pursuing the right thing and being truthful and sincere.

Peace comes from wisdom. And wisdom, as James says in 3:17, is the following:

Pure

Peaceable

Gentle

Open to reason

Full of mercy and good fruits

Impartial

Sincere

"And a harvest of righteousness is sown in peace by those who make peace" (v. 18).

Peace often comes through pain. It's painful to work through our hurts, to humble ourselves and ask for forgiveness when we need to, to put necessary boundaries in place or say no to things that aren't best right now or say yes to things that terrify us because they're so risky. It's the process of working through fears, of shedding all bitterness, jealousy, selfish ambition, worries, and anxieties. Of coming fullhearted to people, and to situations, and not holding back love or clarity. God will give us peace as we do the often-uncomfortable work.

Peace is not a feeling. Sometimes I can make a decision based on how I feel about it. But more often than not, peace comes through the very thing that doesn't feel like peace. It comes from knowing that I sought the Lord, I sought wisdom through godly counsel, and I'm doing the best thing I know to do, in love.

Often when we don't feel peace, that's an invitation for us to be curious before the Lord, asking Him to search our hearts so we can rid ourselves of the anxiety and worry and, once again, receive His true peace.

We can ask, *What's this about, God?*

We want to be people of peace, and we also want to live in places of peace. I believe that we have the power to greatly affect the atmospheres we live in. We all do. You have the power to be a person of peace and bring the presence of peace with you, wherever you go. You also have the power to be a person of anxiety and bring the presence of anxiety with you wherever you go.

What is in you will come out of you, for the good or bad of those around you.

In an article titled "Anxious Emotional Fields," David Lee Jones states,

Psychiatrist Murray Bowen coined the term "emotional field" to describe powerful systematic forces—something akin to electro-magnetic fields. We all know how magnets attract iron particles, and how reversing poles of magnets causes them to repel. The more powerful the magnet, the more "stuck" the particles and the more powerful the repulsion. Although emotional fields are invisible, the ways they influence persons are quite knowable and predictable.

He goes on to say, "In anxious emotional fields, anxiety is both contagious and palpable. You can both feel and 'catch' anxiety from others."[2]

My kids love to play with Magna-Tiles. They're basically primary-colored magnets shaped like squares, rectangles, and triangles that connect together to build anything your imagination can create. My kids will spend hours building castles, houses, car ramps, and rocket ships with these Magna-Tiles. (Truly, they are the best, and if you ever need a gift for a kid, get these! But get the Amazon knock-off ones—there isn't much difference, and they're way cheaper!) These shapes can create amazing buildings, but with the touch of one little finger, you can also knock the whole thing down.

It's the same with the presence we bring into a place. I know you've experienced it before. If someone is full of anxiety—they worry and wonder and diminish and try to control—you feel it. It affects the whole room. They may not even mean to show their anxiety, and they may, in fact, try to push it down, but no matter how hard they try, it's present and causes other people in the room to feel anxious. They are creating an anxious emotional field.

One of my favorite comedians is Trey Kennedy. I live for his little monologues about girls and fall and pumpkin spice lattes! He also has some videos on moms, and one in particular about moms preparing their homes for when guests come. We can be crazy! Pillow fluffing, washing our floorboards even though guests never look at them, running around shouting out commands at everyone, frantically shoving things into closets and cleaning things that haven't ever been cleaned! Obviously, it's exaggerated, but there's truth behind it. That mom makes everyone in her family stressed as she tries to make things look perfect for guests. (I wouldn't know anything about this! My family would never say they've seen me like a tornado trying to get everything done!) Our attitude and actions affect our atmospheres.

But a person of peace is different. Have you ever been in a room where someone comes in who is full of peace? Perhaps their face is naturally light and has no strain, or their pace of walking is slower. They can sit and enjoy other people and the experience and be fully present because their mind isn't anxious about what's next or how to respond or who is thinking what. You can feel the peace exuding from them. And you're attracted to it. You want to be around them. You want to be like them.

And here's the thing. They have peace not because they're hiding their face from their reality, but rather because they're looking their reality straight in the eyes and dealing with it. They aren't pushing unwanted emotions down or unwanted thoughts. Instead, they bring them before the Lord, in total honesty, and work it out with Him. They have truly received the peace that He longs to give us, and they in turn give that gift of peace to us.

When I think of a person of peace, I think of my seminary professor Gerry. He's in his seventies, and during the time I've been studying with him, he has been diagnosed with three different cancers. Early on in my studies, he would teach us with his eyelids taped back because his medicine was causing his eyes to droop.

I can imagine the fear that cancer could have caused him, let alone trying to keep up the pace it takes to be a professor, with eighty hours of work each week. And beyond being a professor, he truly is a pastor to pastors—he pours into so many leaders and pastors on a daily basis.

During our classes, he always has a plan of what to teach and where he's going—the curriculum that needs to be covered—and yet, he always lets the conversations get off topic and go down rabbit trails because he wants the curriculum to truly serve us. How is it relating to our ministries and people in real time? How do we work out these biblical truths with real people, and in our real lives today?

He is patient. Calm. Nothing surprises him. It seems like nothing overwhelms him. We can ask any question, and we will be met with grace and truth.

We meet once a month on Zoom, but the first class of every year we meet in person in Portland. I remember the first time I was in Portland he let us out for a coffee break and our class was going to walk down the road to the local coffee shop to get a delicious, authentic cup of coffee. I asked Gerry if I could get him something, and he just smiled, holding his thermos, and said, "No, I'm okay, Alyssa. I have my good ol' cup of coffee that I brew in my office that's just fine by me."

He is content, calm, and full of lightness. Despite the heavy load he carries in academia, the burdens of those he shepherds, and the trials of his health.

He exudes peace, and it changes the atmosphere of the rooms he enters. He isn't concerned about himself in a fretful manner, but focuses on those right in front of him.

And this can be true of us today. He is a glimpse of what we can become.

It starts now. Today. By sowing into peace, so we can become people of peace.

It's going slow. Not being in a hurry. In our days, with our hearts.

I've started to tell myself when I start to feel like I need to rush, or I'm behind, *Alyssa, go slow. You're not in a hurry. Go at the pace of Jesus.*

Jesus walked everywhere. The average pace of someone who walks is three miles per hour. Imagine if we had to walk everywhere. Wouldn't we be so much more aware of the needs of those around us? So much more aware of our needs inside of us? We would see people better, be more readily available, be able to be interrupted, and not feel like we're in a rush.

I think often we feel anxious because we feel like we're behind. We've missed it and we have to catch up. We're not where we thought we'd be, not where they are. We need to catch up! We need to do the thing, and quick!

Hurry is never helpful; it only zaps all energy and joy.

As Dallas Willard so famously said, "We must ruthlessly eliminate hurry from our lives."[3]

As my husband so poignantly titled his book, "To hell with the hustle!"

Hustle and hurry will only deform us into people of anxiety, rather than transform us into people of peace.

We can only receive the peace God wants to give us when we spend time with Him. We're living in an age where anxiety is the norm. We wake up and we reach for our phones to check the time, turn off our alarms, and then scroll our newsfeed or our IG or check Facebook. We are face-to-face every day with the hardships of others, of our world, with all that we are missing out on and all the *amazing* things that others are doing. The pressure to live up to certain lifestyles or paces of life is uncanny.

Do this.

Be this.

Right now. Today.

It's enough to make us want to just crawl back into bed.

What if we changed the script? What if we were different? What if, instead of going about our days full of anxiety, dread, and worry, we were full of peace, knowing that right where we were was exactly where we were meant to be? That this life, the one we are face-to-face with every day, is, in fact, where God wants us to plant our feet and sow seeds and be fully present? What if our presence was a gift to others? What if our presence was full of love, joy, and peace? What if we were not in a hurry and not worried, fully ready to receive whatever came in a day, knowing that we were not alone and that the outcome didn't rest on our shoulders? Oh yes, we have a big role to play, and oh yes, our presence matters. But our role is to be present and secure and anchored, not frazzled, stressed, and needing to make it all happen.

So how do we live in spaces where other people create atmospheres of anxiety?

We can differentiate from them.

Peter L. Steinke describes *differentiation* in his book *Uproar* like this: "A capacity to be in relationship to others without being ruled by one's own or others' emotional reactivity."[4] He goes on to say later in the book, "The non anxious presence involves engagement, being there and taking the heat if need be, witnessing the pain and yet not fighting fire with fire."[5]

As we anchor ourselves in Jesus, we become steady and peaceful. We do the work, we enter the arena, we love well, but we do so with open hands and open hearts. Open hearts to love others well—full of compassion and empathy and kindness. But we stay calm, we stay peaceful because God is our anchor—not the world, not others. We do not take on the emotional reactivity of others. We can be fully present and fully rooted in Jesus' steadiness.

In order to do this, though, we must first take inventory of our own heart. We have to be self-aware. We have to take time and space to consider how we're doing, why we reacted the way we did, what we're worried about, what needs to be given over to Jesus. If we are not aware of our own hearts, then we cannot show up fully present to care for others. We have to grow and get our roots firmly planted—our sturdiness of soul—so that when the wind comes (and it will), we will not be shaken.

Seeking Jesus first thing in the day grounds us. I'm sure you've heard of the concept of grounding. It's a popular practice right now. Grounding is where you go outside barefoot and walk on the grass or pavement for thirty minutes in order to heal pain, reduce inflammation, and improve your quality of sleep. It also helps to deal with intense anxiety or overwhelming feelings. In a similar fashion, we must seek to ground ourselves in God. To go to Him, barefooted so to speak, perhaps feeling unraveled, and let Him not only heal our pain, reduce our worries, and improve our lives, but actually fill us head to toe with His Spirit that comforts, counsels, intercedes, and reminds us of all that is true.

Eugene Peterson talks about morning and evening prayer in the Psalms. Psalm 4 is an evening prayer, and Psalm 5 is a morning one. He makes this profound statement about our morning prayer:

> The work of God begins while we are asleep and without our help. He continues to work through the day in our worship and obedience. A sacrifice is the material means of assembling a life before God in order to let God work with it. Sacrifice isn't something we do for God, but simply setting out the stuff of life for him to do something with. On the altar the sacrificial offering changed into

what is pleasing and acceptable to God. In the act of offering, we give up ownership and control, and watch to see what God will do with it. With a deep awareness that the God who speaks life into us also listens when we speak, we put into words the difficulties and delights that we foresee in the hours ahead. We assemble fears and hopes, apprehensions and anticipations, and place them on the altar as an offering: "I prepare a sacrifice, and watch."[6]

What if instead of checking our phone first thing in the morning, we stopped and prayed? What if we kept our phones away from us, turned off, or simply put in a drawer, until after we've talked with God? And what if we entered that time asking God, "What do You have for me today? What are You up to that I can join in on?" I wonder what would go differently if we started our days thinking about who God is, reflecting on Psalm 23, and asking how we can join in.

Oh yes, we lay our fears and our worries at His feet. Sometimes we get on our knees with our blanket covering our heads and we pour it out. We cry, we praise, we hope, we grieve. Whatever we feel, whatever season we are in, but we meet with God and look to Him first. We see Him.

This is the way of peace.

Seeking Him first thing, grounding ourselves in Him, we would go about our days with such a different air. We would be full of His peace, no matter what the day entailed, because we would be seeing it through His eyes, and not our own. We would have His eyes to see with compassion, to see the unseen in the ordinary, to make the ordinary beautiful. We would be grounded in Him so we would not lose our footing as we walked on. We would receive this peace that Jesus talks about, peace beyond understanding that

Paul talks about. (John 14:27, Phil. 4:7) We would have inner peace as we walk out into whatever the day holds.

As we sit with Jesus and receive His gift of peace, we can become people of peace. People who can hold pain, and the pain of others, who can hold the anxiety of others without letting it consume us and cause us to be anxious ourselves. We can learn to "carry each other's burdens" (Gal. 6:2 NIV) because we are yoked with Jesus, and not with the burdens themselves.

God does not call us to a life of exhaustion. He doesn't want us to live with heavy burdens and tight chests and hopelessness. He doesn't want us to stay undone.

I know you don't want to live that way either.

But we cannot get ourselves out of the pit of exhaustion and anxiety and hopelessness on our own—no matter how often we cold plunge or take our vitamins or sweat out all our toxins on our exercise bikes!

Those things help us to be healthy, but God alone gives us peace. Because He alone is peace.

The Prince of Peace.

The One who calms the storms, who walks on water, who holds children and eats with tax collectors. The Man who was not rattled by the storm, was not rattled by having no place to lay His head, was not rattled by letting others down, by not living up to their expectations of who they thought He should or would be. He knew who He was as God's Son; He knew His mission; He knew the loving care of the Father and that He was the King and would defeat darkness and have all authority given to Him.

He walked slow. He walked unhurried. He was available. He was present. He was grateful. He was hopeful. He was trusting.

That's not to say He didn't wrestle, He didn't get tired, He didn't experience great pain and temptation. But He knew He was King, and He was coming to inaugurate His kingdom, and He would rise, and "everything would be okay."

Let your exhaustion, your anxiety, be soothed and healed and freed by the One who is Peace.

Spiritual Practice

Take a big breath and exhale. Slow your body down.

Ask God if there's any area of your life that you are living out of worry or hurry or stress. Ask Him what you need to let go of, or implement, to live a more peaceful life. A more unhurried life.

Tell God, "I want to walk at Your pace."

A great practice for becoming a person of peace is Sabbath. For twenty-four hours, if you can—if not, then try two or four hours to start out—rest. Put aside all that you need to do, all that you didn't get to, and just be. Stop doing. Enjoy God. Sleep. Slow. And celebrate. Part of our hurry is that we often think the world depends on us, or that our worth is based on what we can accomplish. Sabbath frees us from those expectations, where we realize God carries the world and our lives, and we get the gift of being His children, and we can rest.

13

CHOOSING JOY

Joy is my middle name. It's also the middle name we gave our old-est daughter, Kinsley. Perhaps because joy was woven into my actual identity, it's a word that I have often clung to and sought after and wrestled with—wrestled with because it baffles me how much I have to fight to have it, how it doesn't come so naturally or stay for as long as I'd like it to.

I want to be a woman of deep joy, and yet often I feel the sorrow of life so close at hand. Happiness evades me more than I'd like.

But perhaps that's the problem. Happiness and joy are not the same. Happiness in the West is immediate gratification, comfort, and satisfaction. Happiness in Jesus is deep and rich and long-lasting. It's joy. America is founded on the pursuit of happiness, and in the West, happiness is our foundational value. Our Western culture shouts from the mountaintops that not only can we be happy, but we should pursue happiness with everything within us. Sacrifice everything for our happiness. And happiness, or flourish-ing, is anything and everything as long as it doesn't cause harm. This is the good life.

Even in the church, we can tend to believe similarly. We can easily believe that we are entitled to a happy life. We can even try to manipulate God into giving us happiness. If He is good, then shouldn't I have a good life?

We expect to live like we were back in Eden, but we can't, because this world is, in fact, fallen and we are broken, so we demand heaven. But we are only left with frustration and anger and despair. We get exhausted from chasing this life of happiness that we are promised, that we feel entitled to. And when the chase does not end with the happiness that we thought, we get disillusioned, and life seems to come apart at the seams.

The problem is that the good life that God wants to give us, with true, lasting, deep joy, often comes through suffering. Joy and sorrow go hand in hand. God does not call us to a life free of pain or hurt, but rather He calls us *through* a life of pain and hurt to discovering true joy. A joy that will never fade. A joy that is not dependent on anyone or anything other than God Himself. This joy is more than happiness. It's better. Happiness comes and goes. And in God's grace, we experience happy moments and happy days. But God's joy remains no matter what the day holds.

Just yesterday my family and I spent the afternoon at the beach. We had fresh peach shakes from Chick-fil-A and the new Jonas Brothers album blasting from our car, the kids singing "Waffle House" from the back seat as we drove to the ocean. The sun was shining, the kids were all getting along, snorkeling, while Jeff and I sat on our beach chairs and read and napped. It was glorious. My mama's heart was so happy.

That was a happy day.

My heart was full, and I was grateful.

However, what do we do on days that are not full of happiness? What do we do in seasons that cause our hearts to utterly break, and when we wake up with eyes swollen from tears shed the night before, and live under the stress of responsibilities and unknowns and trials?

Last year, when we were going through such an anguishing season with homeschool, when I felt like I was losing the fight for my child's heart, I voxed my friend Sara and admitted my doubt and struggle. I locked myself in the closet and told her, "Sara, I don't understand James 1. I just read it today: 'Count it all joy, my brothers, when you meet trials of various kinds, for you know that the testing of your faith produces steadfastness. And let steadfastness have its full effect, that you may be perfect and complete, lacking in nothing.' How do I count this trial a joy? I feel like it's more of a curse."

I couldn't understand how hardships could be a joy, until later. Until months later, as I saw the Lord move and work, slowly, on me. Oh, this hardship, this agonizing pain and day-after-day discouragement where I felt like I was losing heart as a mom, was actually building in me fibers of faith and steadfastness, no matter how long or how hard the battle. Although it felt like it was stripping me and taking away, it, in fact, was building and strengthening me. It's that upside-down kingdom. How pain actually produces beauty, and sorrow actually births joy. So our trials then can be counted as gifts, not curses. *The Message* says it this way: "Consider it a sheer gift, friends, when tests and challenges come at you from all sides. You know that under pressure, your faith-life is forced into the open and shows its true colors. So don't try to get out of anything prematurely. Let it do its work so you become mature and well-developed, not deficient in any way."

Dallas Willard described joy and sorrow coexisting in this way in an interview:

When he [Paul] is describing himself, one of the contrasts he uses is "sorrowful, yet always rejoicing" (2 Corinthians 6:10 NRSV). Joy is consistent with sorrow because it is a realization of what's really going on in the world at large under God. It's joy. You know, it's very difficult to think of God as joyous, because he's got so many things to worry about. But if you don't have a joyous God, you'd better head for cover. Really, you know? It's a joyous God that fills the universe.[1]

Joy and sorrow can go hand in hand. Together. Not separate. I don't say that to make you despair or to fear true joy because sorrow will be close at hand. It's not like you have to fear the other shoe dropping. Rather, it's a truth that should bolster our faith and help us fight against the fear of pain. Pain will come, but we can rest assured that with the pain, there will be joy. Not right away. But eventually. It's only *through* pain that we can experience the deep joy we are longing for. And we can know that as we cry today, He is the God who will wipe our tears and hold us close. Joy will come, but even as we wait for the morning, joy is still with us through the night.

"Joy is not the absence of pain, but the presence of God," said Elisabeth Elliot,[2] a woman who knew pain so deeply with the loss of two husbands and yet lived with utter joy.

Joy is the presence of God, as we sit with Him, learn from Him, walk with Him, and partner with Him. It's having His presence invade every part of our lives, every part of our hearts. And then living differently. Living in His presence.

This is good news! Our joy will not fade with our age, with our life stages, with our seasons, with our circumstances, with our relationships. Because joy is, in fact, a person. Jesus. And it's Jesus with us that fills us with unshakable joy.

But joy can only be experienced, can only be fully accepted, when we sit and spend time with Jesus. When we contemplate His character and His faithfulness and His promises. We must sit and see Jesus in the most beautiful sunshiny days and in the darkest hour of our lives. He is with us in the sorrow and in the good, and both, somehow, are turned into gifts because He uses it all for our transformation, as we behold Him. And then as we behold Him, we go out and make Him known.

When Jeff and I went to New York last December, we spent a morning with Jon Tyson. Jeff and Jon have become fast friends as they have worked together, creating ministries for men to be fully alive, and I have been blessed to spend time with him and glean so much wisdom from our conversations. We were standing outside his favorite bagel shop that December morning, huddled together. You could see our breath in the air and the steam from our sandwiches. I had on my grandpa's black beaver hat (it's actually so cute) from the fifties that I had gotten after his passing and my green puffer jacket, moving my legs back and forth to try to stay warm. Jon was telling us stories of ministry and his life, and I finally gathered the courage I needed to ask him the question that had been burning in my head for months.

"Jon, how do you keep going? In life, in ministry, after so much hard, and yet you're so full of joy. You are always smiling and have this glimmer in your eye."

He smiled and looked at me with that same twinkle in his eye and said in his thick Australian accent, "Alyssa, it's because I have the *bubble of wonduh*" (*wonder*, but, you know, in his Australian accent, it comes off as "wonduh"!).

Bubble of wonder? What was that?

He went on: "How could I not be full of joy? Look at what I get to do on a daily basis. My life is lived on mission; I'm in a war zone and I get to tell people about Jesus. Every day I see pain and crisis, and I also get to see God at work here. And I get to be a part of it. I am so incredibly grateful for my life. For what God has given me. He is so good."

In true New York fashion, he then crumpled his trash up in his hands and started to move along quickly, on to the next stop—coffee. As he and Jeff continued to talk, I followed mulling over those three words: "bubble of wonder." I turned them over and over in my mind. I couldn't stop thinking about them that whole day. I wanted what Jon had. I wanted a bubble of wonder. But how?

I was in my midthirties and had gone through a hard year. The realities of life were staring me straight in my face. Yes, I was still a dreamer and visionary, but I was well aware of the hardships of life these days. Three of my grandparents had passed that year, I had had three friendships dissolve without resolution, and some of my friends had walked away from Jesus. Motherhood was the greatest gift and unbelievably harder than I had ever imagined. I wouldn't say that I was cynical, but I could feel the realities of life start to strangle the awe.

Those three words, "bubble of wonder," became an altar moment. A place where I laid my little stones, stacked high, on the streets of New York next to the bagel shop, where I decided to always seek to be a person of wonder, and not cynicism. No, I would not let the realities of life bring me to apathy, but rather, I would learn to hold both sorrow and joy in a way that called me to "rejoice always" as Paul proclaims in Philippians 4:4. But notice that isn't the whole verse. No, he says to "rejoice in the Lord." *In the Lord*, we can always rejoice. *In the Lord*, we can always have true joy and a heart that is soft to His wonders.

The next day, I texted Jon on our group thread and asked him more about the bubble of wonder. I said, *Okay, how do I get this bubble of wonder? I took away from our conversation that I need to have gratitude, be on mission, and in prayer. Anything else? How do I sow into having more joy?*

His reply was short. *Contemplation. Deep reflection on God's goodness.*

I wonder what would happen if we lived with a bubble of wonder. If we took time to sit and think about God's goodness daily. To deeply soak in His goodness. To us, in His Word, in our communities, in nature.

Joy can only be woven into us through gratitude. Gratitude is what keeps our hearts soft in a world that wants to break us. In a world where sin lives and in bodies where our flesh can war against our spirit. Gratitude takes our eyes off of our circumstances and puts them on the One who is higher than them all. It allows us to notice all the ways He works and is present with us, in the big and the small, the momentous and the ordinary. It shows us the gift it is to have breath in our lungs and hearts that are pumping. Gratitude offers us the opportunity to see things as He sees them, in the unseen. Meeting God in prayer—that is what fills us with joy. As we go to the secret place and sit with Him, the One who holds our sorrow and listens to our cries. And partner with Him in His mission.

God, what are You up to today and how can I be a part of it?

He is at work all around us. He is at work as we sleep. When we wake up in the morning, we are, in fact, joining in on what He's already been doing, not the other way around. He does not join in on what we are doing. No, we get to ask and see how we can be a part of His work.

Jon then sent this quote from theologian J. I. Packer: *"Once you become aware that the main business that you are here for is to know God, most of life's problems fall into place of their own accord."*[3] And as we get to know God more and more, we become more like Him and can't help but live on mission with Him. We can't help but be about the things He's about, have the heart that He has for the lost and hurting, and long to see His kingdom come where we are.

Kinsley has a banner above her bed that says in big bold letters, CHOOSE JOY. We have a choice to choose joy every day, in every moment. Will we choose to think about all that isn't? Will we choose to complain? Will we choose to sit in our woes?

Or will we choose to be thankful? To see with His eyes, to be full of gratitude, even in the hard?

Will we choose to sit with Jesus? To talk with Him about our worries, and pour our hearts out with our sorrows? Will we pray His words back to Him, claiming His promises and His truth as our own? Or will we choose to let the busyness of the day and our to-do lists and our plans cloud out the most important thing? I know I am more of a contemplative and love to just sit and think. I have a monk-like heart but live in a busy world. My favorite mornings are ones where I have hours by myself before anyone is up in my house, where I can pray and journal and read and delight. But I have to fight so hard for those, and they are rarer these days than I'd like. You may be more of a "doer" than me, or more on the go than I am. That's your personality; you are a party just waiting to happen! Regardless of our personalities, and how we're wired, we must seek to be with Jesus. To really set our minds on His goodness, on who He is. To turn and look to Him. The question isn't how; the question is how much is meeting with God worth to you? Will you seek Him, knowing it's Him that your heart is longing for?

We have a choice to choose joy, in the midst of our real lives, not the ones we are wishing for. Will we receive our true lives with joy because we choose to be in constant wonder at who God is and what He does?

Dallas Willard says this about joy:

Joy is the final word. "My joy I give you," Jesus said. Along with his peace and his love came joy. That is based on the reality that things are really better than you can ever imagine as you live in the kingdom of God. You learn that and you have joy. Joy is a pervasive sense of well-being that springs up in the cheer. I love that word cheer. We have associated it with cheerleaders and all sorts of silly stuff, but I love it when Jesus says in the old translations, "be of good cheer." That's where we live in the kingdom of God.[4]

Joy has the last word. And joy is so much better than happiness because it's not about what we get in life or based on how we feel about our lives, but it's a deep sense of well-being regardless of whatever happens, whatever the outcomes may be. It's who we become in the process of the pain, and it's about who we behold as we journey. As we look to Him, as we gaze into His face, we can shine with His glory that nothing on earth can shake because we are in Him, and He is in us, and we are forever in awe of that mystery. Joy is found in the well-being of our souls.

Christ in me, the hope of glory. (Col. 1:27 NIV)

Winn Collier wrote about Eugene Peterson's life in *A Burning in My Bones*. It is my favorite book of all time. Eugene Peterson is one of my spiritual heroes. He was not perfect in any way, but he sought the Lord and remained faithful and poured into so many. He gave Jesus away. And the thing I loved most about the biography was that I felt like I got the gift of knowing Eugene in all his humanity, and getting a glimpse into what it looks like to seek

Jesus and long for Him above fame, above fortune, above success. He longed to be a good husband, a good father, and a pastor to many. And he taught so many of us how to pray. How to be present with Jesus and present with others. Toward the very end of the book, when Eugene is getting ready to pass, Collier paints this picture for us: "Eugene sat in his rocker, an afghan hung over the back. He faced the water, sun warming his face, eyes closed. No movement. No sound. There was only—how do I say it? Joy. Reverence. Wholeness. Contentment. *Holiness*. This was his cell. This was his cathedral."[5]

Joy has the final word. The question is: Will you choose it?

Spiritual Practice

Enter the bubble of wonder.

List out a few things you are thankful for.

Write out one way you are partnering with God on His mission.

Spend a few moments praying. Asking God for your heart cries, rolling your burdens over to Him.

And then spend a moment thinking about the goodness of God to you.

It might take longer than you'd like. It might take a while to get to contemplation. But as you do so, your mind will change, your heart will catch up, and you will be met with joy.

14

RADIATE

In *Becoming Mrs. Lewis*, a historical fiction book about C. S. Lewis's wife named Joy, the author Patti Callahan sweeps you into the story of how Joy lived in an abusive marriage and became best friends with C. S. Lewis through letter writing. She lived in New York, and Lewis in Oxford, and their letters started with her asking questions about her newfound faith from her child's favorite author. (*The Lion, the Witch and the Wardrobe* is one of my all-time favorite children's stories, and it's the movie our family watches every year on Christmas Eve on the projector on our front porch.) They had much in common and quickly became friends. Eventually, her marriage became so bad that she and her husband divorced (her ex-husband immediately married her cousin, whom he had fallen in love with while still married to Joy), and Joy later admitted to falling in love with Lewis. However, it was a long time until he admitted to his feelings, and still longer before the Church of England would let them marry.

While living in England and editing C. S. Lewis's manuscript that eventually became *Till We Have Faces*, Joy had an epiphany. Jack's (C. S. Lewis's) *Till We Have Faces* is a mythical story about Orual and Psyche and shows how the only way we can truly be loved, for love to be true, is to show our real faces, to be "barefaced."

Patti Callahan explains it like this from Joy's perspective in her novel *Becoming Mrs. Lewis*:

> The face I already possessed before I was born was who I was in God all along, before anything went right or went wrong, before I did anything right or wrong, that was the face of my true self. My "bareface." From that moment on, the love affair I would develop would be with my soul. He was already part of me; that much was clear. And now this would be where I would go for love—to the God in me. No more begging or pursuing or needing. It was my false self that was connected to the painful and demanding heart grasping at the world, leading me to despair. Same as Orual. Same as Psyche. Same as all of humanity. Possibly it was only a myth, Jack's myth, that could have obliterated the false belief that I must pursue love in the outside world—in success, in acclaim, in performance, in a man. The Truth: I was beloved of God. Finally I could stop trying to force someone or something else to fill that role. The pain of shattered illusion swept through me like glass blown through a room after a bomb.[1]

Joy has a moment where she realizes that throughout her life, she had tried to put a veil over her face to be accepted, to find love. She felt like she couldn't be her true self, that that wasn't enough, but she had to seek for man's approval, or the accomplishment of the next book (for she was an author as well). No, she realized she was loved by God, with her "bareface," and she could rest with God. He was all she was longing for.

She gave her true self to God and then was able to show her real self to others. To show up alive, not grasping for the things of this world to satisfy her, but rather resting in all that God was in her and to her.

Back in Exodus 33, when Moses is talking to God face-to-face, barefaced, Moses asks God to show him His glory. Moses got to go up to that mountain and see His glory (from behind), and the result was a face that shone. It shone so much that the people feared it, so he wore a veil over his face when he was with the people but took it off when he went to be with God. The result of being with God, of being in His glory, was a literal shining face.

(If you go into an art gallery today and see a picture of Moses, you may see him with actual horns on his head because the Latin word for *veil* is very similar to the Latin word for *horned*, and so people who read the Bible in Latin were confused about this passage and thought it meant Moses had horns.)[2]

This same glory that Moses experienced was given from the Father to Jesus, and then from Jesus to us through the Spirit. But we have an even better glory than Moses. The glory that Moses reflected was coming to an end because it was of the law. It was carved in stone. We, on the other hand, receive the glory of God, who is engraved on our hearts not with ink but with the Spirit, who is the permanent glory. This glory is not going away. We get to see the face of Jesus, with unveiled faces, with our true selves. But as Joy discovered, we can only fully experience this glory and become our true selves if we bring our real selves to Jesus.

Second Corinthians 3:18 says, "And we all, with unveiled face, beholding the glory of the Lord, are being transformed into the same image from one degree of glory to another. For this comes from the Lord who is the Spirit."

God calls us to come and behold Him. And as we look to Him, turning our faces to Him, our eyes on Him, we will reflect Him to the world. Our transformation is not our doing, but it's the Spirit at work within us as we seek Him.

We reflect whom we revere.

Moses revered God and resembled His light.

The Israelites revered their golden calf and resembled its character—stiff-necked, not hearing, not seeing.

What will we revere?

We get to look to Jesus, behold His glory, and resemble His image—from one glory to another.

It's not us becoming a better version of ourselves as the world likes to claim; it's even more. It's us becoming more like *Jesus*. Transformed into His image. From one glory to another. Often-times in Christian circles, we say, "I'm just a frail human, a broken vessel." Yes, we are frail, weak, and we have limitations. Yes, we are broken, and we hold His treasure in our jars of clay. But He wants to fill our jar of clay with His glory! He wants to fill us with all His fullness, to fill us with His love, His power, His wisdom, His goodness, His grace. He restores our brokenness; he heals us and mends us. He gives strength to the weak. He gives power to the needy. The same Spirit who raised Jesus from the dead lives in you and me! He wants to fill us with all of Himself. We may be a jar of clay, but we are His treasure. And we embody His glory.

His glory is His fullness. It's the weight of His goodness and love and grace and holiness. His glory is so magnificent—it's heavy with meaning and importance. And He has given us His whole self. He's held nothing back. Jesus risked it all, was utterly vulnerable, secure in the Father's love, so that we can now cry out with Moses, "Lord, show us Your glory!"

God wants to give you His whole self. He wants to fill you with all of Him.

We just need to make room for Him.

When we lay down our idols of control and comfort and approval, when we walk with God through the utter devastations and losses of our lives, we aren't left empty-handed and alone.

We're tempted to believe that will be the cost. But when we actually surrender to Him, coming to Him again and again, He gives us the best gift of all—Himself. And it is Him that our hearts are truly longing for.

Our suffering, our exhaustion over trying to manage everything, is an invitation for us to find Jesus and learn to lean in to Him. It's at the end of ourselves where we find Him. It's when we realize we actually can't control the outcomes that we finally come and rest in Him. And we find what our souls are most longing for. We find our deepest desires. What we were made for. Connection to God and becoming a person of love.

And it's here in His presence that we find His utter love and care and delight for us. We learn to not just survive but to relate. We find that life is not dependent upon our performance and our doing and holding it all together. But it's about being held by the One who holds all things together and welcoming others into the family.

We don't need to fear the losses, the weakness, the limitations, the suffering, because "perfect love casts out fear" (1 John 4:18). There is no fear any longer because we come to find that God is actually after our hearts, just as they are, and He offers us His heart always.

It's the only thing that will ever be unconditional. It's the only thing that can ever be fully depended on and surrendered to that won't let us down. Yes, there will be times when we feel let down by God, disappointed, but even those times are invitations to go deeper, to find Him in those disappointments and realize yet again that His love truly satisfies and strengthens us.

Saint Irenaeus said, "The glory of God is a man [or woman] fully alive."[3]

We all long to be fully alive. The problem is that being fully alive

is painful at times. It's often through suffering that we are trans-
formed. It's through being honest with our real desires, our real
pains, and our true realities that we can prevent our hearts from
becoming numb and asleep. It's through coming to Jesus with our
true hearts where we meet Him and are given His fullness, and a
full heart. It's only in His love that we can become fully alive. It's
only by giving Him our true selves that we can receive His love for
our real lives.

We all know about the resurrection of Jesus in John 20, where
Jesus defeats darkness and death and the enemy and defeats all
odds and rises from the dead! And in His resurrection, we are
saved. We are rescued. We can rise to life too! The New Testament
goes further to give us a picture of a resurrection triangle, which
we live in the middle of. We go from John 20 to Revelation 20,
which tells us of the general resurrection of the dead in the future.
But then there's Colossians 3, where we live now, today. Almost in
the valley of these two mountains. And Colossians 3 tells us how
we have already been raised from the dead as believers, so we can
experience the power of God as we live here on earth walking in
our newness of life *today*. And as Eugene Peterson states, "When
[Paul] wrote about being raised with Christ, he was talking about
a miracle. But the miracle isn't that we're delivered from our pres-
ent circumstances; it's that we're transformed through them."[4]

And we are transformed wholly. In mind, body, and heart. God
wants to make us fully alive in all these areas.

He wants to make our minds fully alive. To redeem our imag-
inations. To use our thoughts to think about what is good, lovely,
and praiseworthy. To use our minds to think about the goodness
of God, to give thanks, to meditate on God's character, to use our
minds to hear God's voice, to marvel at His mysteries and won-
ders, to think deeply about His truth and His grace.

He wants to make our bodies fully alive. To have them fully surrendered to Him. He wants us to walk in purity and holiness. To take care of our bodies so we can fully operate in the ways God has gifted us and show up fully and love well. We love through our bodies, through our presence. By being fully present, undistracted, listening, encouraging, speaking life and truth, praying for others. By a hug, a warm meal, freshly folded laundry, a bouquet of flowers picked from our garden, a high five. We receive and we give love through our bodies. But in order to do that, we must be fully surrendered to Him, drenched in His goodness.

He wants to make our hearts fully "live." He wants us to sit and be with Jesus, to learn to live in the unforced rhythms of grace. To not seek approval or performance or success to earn love, but to do what God has called us to do out of His great love for us and our great love for the world. To have our hearts secure in Him, no matter how disorientating or grieving the season. To be secure in His love, that which will never fade or change and can be totally depended upon. We can love others; we can create emotional space for others as our hearts are fully surrendered to Him.

When these three—our minds, our bodies, and our hearts—are aligned with God, people notice. A person fully alive is rare, unusual.

Most people are seeking survival, not fullness.

God's fullness in us, His glory in us, is almost palpable to others. It's something they can pinpoint and see and be in wonder about. But we have to experience it first and then become it. The more we sit with God, absorbed in who He is and in His presence, the more He comes out of us, in our thoughts, in our deeds, in our actions.

The world will tell us that in order to shine, we must do more.

God tells us in order to shine, we must sit more. Sit and be with

Him. Sit and absorb Him. Sit and wonder. Sit and grieve. Sit and ask. Sit and delight.

It's in seeking Him, looking to Him, that we become more like Him.

And it's in our becoming that we get to offer ourselves as a living sacrifice to others. No, we cannot manage the outcomes. We cannot control what happens and how people respond and how it's all going to play out. There are no guarantees.

But there is a guarantee in spending time with Jesus. You will become full of Him. You will be transformed. You will be strengthened and toughened and softened. You will reflect Him. And in becoming more like Him, in all His glory, your presence will become a great gift to those around you. A gift of love, empathy, joy, wonder, confidence, security, grace, kindness, truth, faithfulness, and grace. You cannot control how things play out, but you can influence others by your very presence of groundedness and delight in Jesus.

This summer we had two families stay with us that are dear friends. Friends that we partner with and work together with, friends who are mentors and teachers to us, and whom we just adore. Their teenage and adult kids came too, and we delighted in each other's presence, having bonfires and swim parties and pizza nights.

One night, we threw a dinner party for all of them, setting up a long table by our pool with linen tablecloths and navy-and-tan taper candles and sea-glass wineglasses. We had string lights above us and basked in good food and good company.

While the sun set, Jeff asked everyone this question: "What has been the hardest year of your life and the greatest year of your life?"

What a question!

In true Alyssa form, I went last, as I always need more time to think and process. I was honest about how this past year had been one of my hardest, with all my friendship losses and misunderstandings and not having closure. And then, I was struck with how grateful I was for the year, because I experienced the friendship of the Lord in such deep, intimate ways that I'd never experienced. I experienced wonder in the midst of pain. I experienced a strengthening of soul and was overcome by how the Lord surrounded me with people who deeply love me and can speak truth to me in love and walk with me through pain. I really don't feel like the same person, because I've learned to be with Jesus and sit with Him and hear His voice that loves me.

Jeff agreed out loud that I wasn't the same, and then one of our friends who was there, John, concurred.

"Alyssa, I agree. I know I don't know you super well, but you are not the same from when we were here eighteen months ago. You were lovely then, but now you are strong and secure. I see it on you. Even your voice is different."

I did not know I was changing as time passed. It was not palpable to me. But as I have learned to walk with Jesus, hand in hand, offering my heart to Him in honesty, spending time with Him, slowing down and assessing my heart and thoughts and confessing and receiving, seeking wisdom from counselors and mentors and friends, I have been changed.

And I am longing for more and more glory. To be full of more and more of Him. To get to age eighty and live with a smile on my face, peace in my body, and hope for the future. I long to be a loving presence because I rest in the loving presence of God. I long to look forward to the future with great hope as Proverbs 31:25 says, because I know that God's miracle isn't that we're delivered from pain but that we are transformed through it.

And in His upside-down kingdom, that comes from resting in His presence, not from doing. The doing will come, but only after we sit with Him.

Watchman Nee has a book called *Sit, Walk, Stand* based on the book of Ephesians. In it, he argues that we must learn to sit with Jesus and find our identity in Him. Then we can walk with Him, obeying Him and following in His footsteps, and finally we can stand against the enemy. But we cannot stand until we've learned to sit, and we cannot walk until we've learned to stand. There's no formula, but there is a framework.

Sit with Jesus. Behold His face. Be full of wonder for Him. Lay it all out in His presence, knowing that He wants your heart most of all.

Walk with Jesus. Learn how He walked, see how He does it. Live with grace and kindness and joy. Try softer. Go out and make Him known! Tell everyone about Him. Disciple. Fight back the darkness with goodness, love, mercy, and justice. Stay the course. Remain faithful. He is with you. Always, until the end of time. Stand with Jesus, against the enemy of your soul. You are not a coward; you are not a victim of your circumstances. You are a daughter of the King, who has been given authority and agency to fight against the enemy and his lies.

Spiritual Practice

You can come to Jesus barefaced, just as you are. Every day. Morning by morning, evening by evening. You don't have to change your circumstances, or even change yourself. But you can seek your own spiritual formation by seeking Jesus honestly and openly.

Hear Him whispering today to *come*—and not just come to lay down but come to receive. He wants to fill you with all of His fullness. He wants to increase your capacity for Him, in your present reality.

Sit with Him now, and ask Him these two questions:

1. "Lord, what do You want to do in me relating to (something that may be heavy on your heart)?"
2. "What are You speaking to me?"

Write these down so you can go back to them.

Whatever heavy burden you may be holding, it is an opportunity for God to do His good work in you. And as He works in you, He is drawing you close to His heart.

He longs for your heart, and He longs to give you all of His.

CONCLUSION

Dallas Willard said, "If you don't come apart for a while, you'll come apart after a while."

When we don't take time to get away and hear from Jesus, whether in the busyness and distractions of life or the disappointments that leave us heartbroken, we will find ourselves coming apart. A bit unraveled. Shaky and insecure.

Life is full of outcomes that are out of our control, no matter how hard we try to change them or hold them together. And in the trying to hold all the things together, we can find ourselves coming undone.

But what if God doesn't want us to hold it all together or expect us to get it together?

What God wants is your heart most of all. It is of utmost importance to Him. To have access to your heart, to know your heart, to fill your heart with all of His fullness.

He wants your heart to be fully alive. It is His glory. His glory in you, and His glory pouring out of you.

But in order to do that, we must tend to our hearts. We must take time to create space for us to connect with our hearts.

How am I doing?

What am I feeling?

What am I thinking about?

We must give access to the Lord.

Lord, is there any part of me that I'm withholding from You? Any part that I'm living in fear, or in lies, or out of my wounds?

He wants to give you strength of heart. But that strength must come through adversity, through coming barefaced before the Lord and letting Him shine in our hearts.

He wants to fill you with His love, give you His peace, and satisfy you with His joy. And that comes by approaching Him with an open heart, receiving all that He has, and oftentimes, it is through the loss of relationships, difficult circumstances, and the hardships of life that we realize it is indeed Jesus and His love, peace, and joy that we desire the deepest, not the glory of this world—the success, the approval, the likability, the comfort, the accomplishments. Often, it's when we lose things on earth that we realize we have gained the greatest treasure in Him.

Oh, Jesus, it is You that we long for.

Not to have secured outcomes. Not to try to control and obtain what we think is best and rest in our abilities. That is futile and will only leave us feeling exhausted. It's in entering Jesus' presence that we find all that our hearts are longing for. And we find ourselves to be secure of soul.

The good life comes as we look to Him, at His face, and hear His voice and find the security and the love that we are most after.

But how do we do this in our daily lives? In the busyness, the chaos, the stress, the mundane?

We find time and space to get away with Him. To connect with our hearts. To connect with Him. Silence, solitude, prayer.

It's in the minutes we lie in bed before getting up that we recite the Lord's Prayer and enter our day, surrendered to Him and trusting Him with whatever the day brings. Word, truth, surrender.

It's in the resisting our phones and asking God, "What do You want me to know today?" And listening to whatever it may be, knowing His voice is always one of love, kindness, grace, and truth, not condemnation or shame or pressure.

It's in the time we get ready for the day, asking the Lord to prepare our hearts. Reciting Scripture to ourselves. Praying for others. Clothing ourselves with love, joy, humility, and strength.

It's in the way we serve others through our work—the cooking of a meal, the helping with homework, the emails, the texts, the meetings, the driving, the listening, the playing—showing up fully where we are, knowing this is right where God wants us. We don't have to come all put together; we come barefaced, knowing we are fully loved and secure in Jesus. We come asking, "Lord, what do You want me to know about this person? How do You see them?" And we love them like Jesus.

It's in the time we actually get reading the Word, praying, processing, delighting. Whether it's while on a walk, sitting at a coffee shop, laying out in the sun, stopping to read before we dive back into our work and asking, "Lord, speak. Your servant is listening. Come, Holy Spirit."

It's in the moments between all the things that we simply stop our minds and say, "I receive You now, Lord."

It's in the little moments that we stop and face Jesus and let Him shine on us. When we turn our faces toward Him, and He turns His face toward us.

It's learning that He is indeed present with us all throughout the day, but we must become aware of and awake to Him.

It's walking relationally with the God of the universe and living in surrender because you know He is trustworthy, and loving, and so merciful and kind. He's just. He hates sin. But He convicts us with His utter kindness and welcomes us into the light.

So come into the light, friends. Come gaze on His face. Turn toward Him.

Not your to-do list.

Not your phone.

Not your boss.

Not your inner critic.

Not your strong desires.

Not your shoulds or coulds.

But gaze upon Him, the One who will fulfill all your deepest desires and who will transform you from one degree of glory to another.

A prayer of consecration:

Lord, I look to You now.

I receive all that You have for me.

I want to know You.

I want to know Your love.

I open up my heart to You.

I make room for You.

Do all that is in Your heart to do, Jesus.

I trust You. I am surrendered to You.

I lay down my hopes, my dreams, my pains, my hurts before
*   Your feet.*

Make something beautiful with them. With me.

Make me into Your likeness.

Shine on me, Jesus, with the brightness of Your face, with the
*   fullness of Your glory.*

Show me Your glory.

Fill me with Your fullness.

I am Yours.

You are mine.

Amen.

ACKNOWLEDGMENTS

I am always reminded of how it takes a village to write a book. Although it is one of the greatest privileges of my life, it would not be completed, nor would I be kept whole, without all of those who have faithfully walked with me, supported me, and strengthened me through the process. How does one pour out their heart and soul and story on paper without the community of believers holding them throughout?

There are so many to thank, so in no particular order, and knowing I won't be able to mention everyone who has been such a kindness to me, here it goes:

Thank you to my dearest friends and mentors and warriors in Sisterhood. It's in a huge part because of your lives, your experiences and wisdom and encouragement that I am not the same girl I was four years ago, that this book could even be written to tell a story of a girl who is learning to come to Jesus barefaced and made strong through the ebbs and flows of life and ministry. You all have shown me how it's God's kindness that leads us to repentance, to go slow, to tend to my heart, and how to hold onto hope. Thank you for your prayers of joy, for the countless hours of helping me brainstorm and process and for making me laugh so hard I spit water all over the dinner table. You are one of the greatest treasures of my life.

Emilie, thank you for walking all of life's sorrows and joys with me. You are the sweetest answer to prayer in my life and have shown me how to be honest before God and others and receive all His grace. You are wise, exuberant, and courageous. Also, I'm glad we called a truce on our cold-plunge challenge!

Tammy, thank you for not only creating encounters with Jesus with me, but for genuinely caring for my heart and breathing such life and courage into my soul. Your intentionality and sincerity and love has been the goodness of God to me.

Gerry Breshears, it has been one of the highlights of my life to learn under your wisdom, knowledge, and care these last two years. What a joy to study the Bible together, to work through the mysteries of God and complexities of life, and to come away more in love with God and the church than before. I will never see the Bible the same, knowing the war we are in, the mission we are called to, the compassion of God, and the great longing for hope and healing for all mankind. Thank you for reading my manuscript and giving feedback and being a covering for me. And really for being a pastor and shepherd to me. You are one of the great saints that I will forever be marked by and spurred on by.

Jon Tyson, that night on your rooftop balcony with you, Jeff, and Christy not only radically changed my perspective on the sacred life, but gave me the courage and power to write this book. Thank you for processing it with me, for letting me ask all the questions and wrestle with the content and for your constant "nuggies" of truth that you have fed my soul. Our generation is blessed to have your teaching and preaching which reflects your consecration unto the Lord. Thank you for your apostolic voice and for continuing to run with integrity and humility.

Joel Mudamalle and the Compel Team, thank you for not only being a sounding board for this book idea, but for your direction, encouragement, help, and focus. Wow, you guys are incredible! I felt like you took my book as your own and so generously poured out all you had to make it the best it could be. You all are incredible at what you do, and it was an honor to be part of your team for the day. Joel, I could have sat under your teaching and theology for hours. Thank you for helping me find the theological foundation for this book.

To Rick, my counselor. So much of what is said here is because of the deposits you have made into my life. Thank you for your fatherly care, for how you create space for me to process and let it out, for helping me untangle my emotions and find sturdiness of soul. Even more than what you have said (which is gold) is your presence of love and peace that have shown me God's heart. Thank you for pouring out your care to so many and giving us the tools to handle the hardships of life.

Beth, what a joy it has been to work alongside you with this book! It has been such an honor to have your insight and you have been such an encouragement to me as you get a front row seat at my insecurities and musings and doubts. So many times when I was pulling out my hair wondering, "is this any good!?" you would get me out of the pit, help me problem solve, and wipe my knees off again to keep going. You are so gifted at what you do; thank you for working with me.

Karen, I would not be here without you! Jeff and I are constantly in awe and grateful to be part of the Yates family. Thank you for your friendship, your support, and discernment. Thank you for constantly going to bat for me, for hearing my heart and desires, for helping me meet deadlines and stay on track. Thank you for coaching me through each book with wisdom, grace, and care. It is an honor to have you as an agent, and even more to have you as a friend.

Mom, you have always encouraged me in my writing, and cheered me on, from my second grade Turkey story for "Reflections" to all of my college admission papers. Once again, you faithfully read almost every chapter (the ones I'd give you!) and provided feedback, encouragement, and help. Your gifting is in the details, and I am ever so thankful for how you helped shape this book. Thank you for breathing courage into my writing. I am a reader and writer because of your encouragement in my life.

Jeff, I would not have been able to write any of this if it weren't for your support and help. Thank you for the countless hours you held down the fort so I could go hide away and write in my pajamas until midafternoon or get away to my favorite coffee shop and write till my eyes glazed over. Seminary and a book were no easy task, but you made it possible. Thank you for the endless conversations of me seeking your wisdom because I truly think you are one of the smartest people I know. Thank you for believing in the book, in me and what God is doing, more than I did a lot of days. You get a front row seat at my formation, and I know it's not always easy, but thank you for loving me, choosing me, and spurring me on toward Jesus day by day. You are exactly who I need, and I would choose you over and over. Also, thank you for sending me away to Bend for a week. It was glorious and so much of what's written in these pages is because of how God met me there. I love you forever.

Shannon and Kiara, thank you for flying to Maui to care for my kids so I could write! Goodness, it is a gift to have someone not only love your kids, but make it so fun for them. You two are both such gifts in my life, and were highlights for our whole family in 2023.

Shannon, you are one of the greatest cheerleaders in my life. Thank you for binge-watching *The Summer I Turned Pretty* with me and eating Rice Krispies every night and introducing me to my red light. Your story is still unfolding, and in the hands of Jesus, I know it will be good.

Thank you to my early readers who read my very rough drafts, sacrificed their time, and provided such keen insight. You helped breathe life into these pages. (Thank you, Bianca, for printing out my chapters and writing your thoughts in the margins—I felt so loved!) One day I hope to be in a room with you all to hear your stories and worship together.

And to my Good Shepherd, you have been faithful and true. You are worthy of it all. Thank you for the gift of partnering with You in Your good work and for the joy of Your presence. Lord Jesus, come. May your Kingdom come, your will be done, on earth as it is in heaven. To You be all glory and fame. I love You.

NOTES

Introduction

   1 Eugene Peterson, *A Long Obedience in the Same Direction* (Lisle: IVP, 2021).

Chapter 1

   1 Sissy Goff, *Raising Worry-Free Girls* (Bloomington: Bethany House Publishers, 2019), 38.

   2 Arlie Hochschild, *The Managed Heart* (Oakland: University of California Press, 2012).

   3 Dane Ortlund, *Gentle and Lowly: The Heart of Christ for Sinners and Sufferers* (Wheaton: Crossway, 2020), 20–21.

   4 Blue Letter Bible, https://www.blueletterbible.org/lexicon/g373/esv/mgnt/0-1/.

Chapter 2

   1 John Eldredge, *Waking the Dead: The Secret to a Heart Fully Alive* (Nashville: Thomas Nelson, 2016).

   2 Peter Scazzero, *Emotionally Healthy Spirituality* (Grand Rapids: Zondervan, 2017).

   3 Geri Scazzero, *The Emotionally Healthy Woman: Eight Things You Have to Quit to Change Your Life* (Grand Rapids: Zondervan, 2014), 77.

   4 Ortlund, *Gentle and Lowly* (Wheaton: Crossway, 2020), 18.

   5 Dallas Willard, *Renovation of the Heart* (Colorado Springs: NavPress, 2021), 28.

Chapter 3

   1 David Benner, *Desiring God's Will* (Wheaton: InterVarsity Press, 2015), 76.

   2 Cornelius Plantinga Jr., *Not the Way It's Supposed to Be: A Breviary of Sin* (Grand Rapids: Eerdmans Publishing, 1996), 9.

3 John Mark Comer, "The Deep Desire to Be with God," *Art of Teaching* podcast, Youtube.

4 Comer, "The Deep Desire to Be with God," *Art of Teaching* podcast, Youtube.

5 John Eldredge, *The Journey of Desire: Searching for the Life You've Always Dreamed Of* (Nashville: Thomas Nelson, 2016), 15.

6 Eldredge, *The Journey of Desire* (Nashville: Thomas Nelson, 2016), 13.

7 Benner, *Desiring God's Will* (Wheaton: InterVarsity Press, 2015), 82.

8 Eldredge, *The Journey of Desire* (Nashville: Thomas Nelson, 2016), 13.

Chapter 4

1 John Piper, "To Live Is Christ—What Does That Mean?," December 13, 2017, DesiringGod.org, *Ask Pastor John* podcast, episode 1132, https://www.desiringgod.org/interviews/to-live-is-christ-what-does-that-mean#:~:text=So%20again%2C%20"to%20live%20is,magnificent%20as%20your%20supreme%20treasure.

2 C. S. Lewis, *Mere Christianity* (San Francisco: HarperOne, 2023), 180.

3 C. S. Lewis, *The Lion, the Witch and the Wardrobe* (New York: Harper Collins, 2002).

Chapter 5

1 *Oxford English Dictionary*, s.v. "control (v.)," September 2023, https://doi.org/10.1093/OED/6632095569.

2 *Cambridge Dictionary*, "control (v.)," https://dictionary.cambridge.org/us/dictionary/english/control.

3 Jon Tyson, *The Burden Is Light* (Colorado Springs: Multnomah, 2018), 64.

4 Tyson, *The Burden is Light*, 76.

5 M. Robert Mulholland Jr. *Invitation to a Journey* (Westmont: IVP, 2016).

6 Sissy Goff, David Thomas, and Melissa Trevathan, *Are My Kids on Track?* (Bloomington: Bethany House Publishing, 2017).

Chapter 6

1 Bob Sorge, *Dealing with the Rejection and Praise of Man* (Grandview: Oasis House Publishing, 1999).

2 Trevor Hudson, *Beyond Loneliness*, 54.

3 Hudson, *Beyond Loneliness*, 54.

4 Gary Moon, *Becoming Dallas Willard* (Westmont: IVP, 2018).

5 Sorge, *Dealing with the Rejection and Praise of Man* (Grandview: Oasis House Publishing, 1999).

Chapter 7

1 Michael Easter, *The Comfort Crisis* (Emmaus: Rodale Books, 2021), 5.
2 *Comfort Crisis.* 48.
3 *Comfort Crisis.* 50.
4 St. Augustine, *City of God* (London: Penguin Classics, 2004).
5 John Ortberg, *The Life You've Always Wanted* (Grand Rapids: Zondervan, 2015).

Chapter 8

1 Merriam-Webster.com, "ideal," https://www.merriam-webster.com/dictionary/ideal.
2 Larry Crabb, *Shattered Dreams* (Colorado Springs: WaterBrook, 2010), 44.
3 Crabb, *Shattered Dreams*, 13.

Chapter 9

1 Lysa TerKeurst, *It's Not Supposed to Be This Way* (Nashville: Thomas Nelson, 2018).

Chapter 10

1 https://www.apa.org/topics/grief#:~:text=Grief%20is%20the%20anguish%20experienced,death%20of%20a%20beloved%20person.
2 Jon Tyson, "We Want You Here: Praying Through Tears" podcast, May 28, 2023.
3 Ungolino di Monte Santa Maria, Evelyn Underhill, John F. Thornton, *The Little Flowers of St. Francis of Assisi* (New York: Vintage Spiritual Classic, 1998).
4 Ann Voskamp, "What Do You Do with All This Grief," Ann Voskamp.com, 2022, https://annvoskamp.com/2022/05/what-do-you-do-with-all-of-this-grief/#readpost.
5 Eugene Peterson, *The Message Devotional Bible* (Colorado Springs: NavPress, 2018).
6 Eugene Peterson, *Answering God* (San Francisco: HarperOne, 1991), 100.
7 Ann Voskamp, *The Broken Way* (Nashville: Thomas Nelson, 2016).
8 Jon Tyson, "We Want You Here: Praying Through Tears," May 28, 2023.
9 C. S. Lewis, *The Great Divorce* (San Francisco: Harper One, 2015).

Chapter 11

1 G. K. Beale, *Union with the Resurrected Christ* (Ada: Baker Academic, 2023), 281.
2 David G. Benner, *Surrender to Love: Discovering the Heart of Christian Spirituality* (Westmont: IVP, 2015), 74.
3 John Ortberg, *Soul Keeping* (Grand Rapids: Zondervan, 2014).
4 Benner, *Surrender to Love* (Westmont: IVP, 2015), 76.

Chapter 12

1 *Blue Letter Bible*, Blueletterbible.org, https://www.blueletterbible.org/lexicon/g1515/esv/mgnt/0-1/.
2 David Lee Jones, "Anxious Emotional Fields—Family Systems Theory for Church Leaders," *The Presbyterian Outlook*, October 24, 2017 (updated September 9, 2022), Pres-outlook.org/2017/10/anxious-emotional-fields-family-systems-theory-church-leaders/.
3 Dallas Willard, *Living in Christ's Presence: Final Words on Heaven and the Kingdom of God* (Westmont: IVP, 2017).
4 Peter L. Steinke, *Uproar: Calm Leadership in Anxious Times* (Lanham: Rowan and Littlefield Publishers, 2019).
5 Steinke, *Uproar* (Lanham: Rowan and Littlefield Publishers, 2019), 51.
6 Peterson, *Answering God* (San Francisco: Harper One, 1991), 66.

Chapter 13

1 Willard, *Living in Christ's Presence* (Westmont: IVP, 2017), 81.
2 Elisabeth Elliot, *Suffering Is Never for Nothing* (Nashville: B & H, 2019).
3 J. I. Packer, Knowing God (Westmont: IVP, 1993).
4 Willard, *Living in Christ's Presence* (Westmont: IVP, 2017), 81.
5 Winn Collier, *A Burning in My Bones* (Colorado Springs: WaterBrook, 2022), 306.

Chapter 14

1 Patti Callahan, *Becoming Mrs. Lewis* (Nashville: Thomas Nelson, 2020), 324.
2 N. T. Wright, *Paul for Everyone: 2 Corinthians* (Minnetonka: Westminster John Knox Press, 2004), 35.
3 Peter Scazzero, *Emotionally Healthy Spirituality* (Grand Rapids: Zondervan, 2017), 26.
4 Eugene Peterson, *The Message Devotional Bible* (Colorado Springs: NavPress, 2018).

ABOUT THE AUTHOR

Alyssa Joy Bethke loves Jesus, matcha, and the sun, and squeezes as much pickleball and reading into her week as possible. She is married to Jeff, the love of her life, and is mom to three of the greatest gifts: Kinsley, Kannon, and Lucy. The Bethke family recently moved from Maui to Tennessee and are embracing the wild adventure of a life surrendered to God. Alyssa and Jeff help reclaim God's design for men, women, and families at Forming Men, Forming Women, and Family Teams.